Fleet in Focus
HOULDER'S POST-WAR GRA~~~~~
John B. Hill

The post-war fleet

1. DUNSTER GRANGE 1928-1951 Twin-screw refrigerated cargo ship
O.N. 149981 9,494g 6,011n 453.0 x 64.5 x 31.1 feet.
Two Fairfield-Sulzer type 6-cyl. 2SCSA oil engines by Fairfield Shipbuilding and Engineering Co. Ltd., Govan driving twin screws; 6,400 BHP, 15 knots.
Insulated capacity 556,840 cubic feet.
12 passengers.
25.10.1927: Launched by Fairfield Shipbuilding and Engineering Co. Ltd., Govan (Yard No. 622) for Houlder Line Ltd. (Houlder Brothers and Co. Ltd., managers), London as DUNSTER GRANGE.
20.1.1928: Completed.
27. 12 1951: Sold to Vassan Laiva O/Y, Vasa, Finland for £325,000 and renamed VASA.
1958: Sold to Hokuyo Suisan K.K., Tokyo, Japan, converted into a fish meal factory and renamed KINYO MARU.
1963. Sold to Nippon Suisan K.K., Tokyo, converted into a crab factory ship and renamed YOKO MARU.
25.5.1974: Arrived for demolition at Aioi, Japan in tow from Innoshima, having been sold to Taiyo Kaiji Kabushiki Kaisha, Osaka.

2. RIPPINGHAM GRANGE 1943-1961 Twin-screw refrigerated cargo ship
O.N. 169564 10,365g 4,239n 464.5 x 65.5 x 27.5 feet.
Two Werkspoor type 8-cyl. 4SCSA oil engines by Hawthorn Leslie and Co. Ltd., Newcastle-upon-Tyne driving twin screws; 6,700 BHP, 15 knots.
Insulated capacity 556,370 cubic feet.
24 passengers. Later altered to 12, in single berth cabins.
6.3.1943: Launched by Hawthorn, Leslie and Co. Ltd., Hebburn-on-Tyne (Yard No. 653) for Houlder Line Ltd. (Houlder Brothers and Co. Ltd., managers), London as RIPPINGHAM GRANGE.
28. 9.1943: Delivered.
4.9.1961: Sold to Far East Marine Enterprises (Moller and Co.), Hong Kong for £140,000 and renamed ABBEY WOOD.
23.4.1962: Arrived at Hakodate, Japan for demolition by the Hakodate Dock Co. Ltd., Hakodate. Sold with one main engine inoperable due to bearing damage, which occurred on her last commercial voyage, and sailed in this condition to Japan.
5.1962: Work commenced

The war-time built refrigerator ship *Rippingham Grange.*
[Fotoflite incorporating Skyfotos, author's collection]

Top: *Urmston Grange* was refrigerated in numbers 2 and 3 holds. *[A Duncan, author's collection]*

Middle: *Ovingdean Grange* photographed at Montevideo in December 1946 with her original, narrow, wartime funnel, a white forecastle, and a white band on her hull. *[J. and M. Clarkson]*

Bottom: *Ovingdean Grange* on 22nd July 1950 with a 'proper' funnel. *[F.W. Hawks, author's collection]*

Opposite: *Langton Grange* in the Thames. *[World Ship Photo Library]*

CONTENTS

Ships in Focus Publications

Correspondence and editorial:
Roy Fenton
18 Durrington Avenue
London SW20 8NT
020 8879 3527
rfenton@rfenton.demon.co.uk

Orders and photographic:
John & Marion Clarkson
18 Franklands, Longton
Preston PR4 5PD
01772 612855
sales@shipsinfocus.co.uk
© 2002 Individual contributors,
John Clarkson and Roy Fenton.

Printed by Amadeus Press Ltd., Cleckheaton, Yorkshire.
Designed by Hugh Smallwood, John Clarkson and Roy Fenton.
SHIPS IN FOCUS RECORD
ISBN 1 901703 17 7

SHIPS IN FOCUS RECORD 20
June 2002

Looking back from Issue 20 - something of a landmark - the editors remind themselves that *Record* was conceived as an illustrated journal, and the inclusion of photo features on ports such as Aberdeen in issue 18, Sunderland in 19 and Irish harbours in this issue and the next is central to our philosophy. Although we have sufficient articles in hand or under development for at least the next three issues, we would like more of these port pictorials. Can you help? Do you have photographs of a particular port, or know of a good collection in a local museum or library from which prints can be obtained? Ideally, we would welcome detailed captions to accompany the photographs, but if you do not feel capable of writing them yourself, we should be able to find someone to help. As always, we would ask aspiring contributors to drop us a line before starting work.

Our announcement of new arrangements for binding *Record* in the last issue left some readers confused as to how many they could have bound in one volume. Although *Record* issues are numbered individually (largely because we took some time to arrive at our current quarterly publishing interval), four issues are considered to make up a volume. The pages in these four issues are numbered consecutively, and the fourth issue (such as this) has eight 'bonus' pages of which four are given over to an index for the notional volume. So, the binders will bind four issues into a volume: 1 to 4, 5 to 8, 9 to 12, 13 to 16, and now 17 to 20. To remind you, the bookbinder is Ken Toft Bookbinders, Unit 4, Brassey Street (off Laird Street), Birkenhead, CH41 8BY. The charge for binding each volume is £16 plus £4 postage. Four copies of *Record* bound in this way make a very handsome book.

John Clarkson   Roy Fenton

SUBSCRIPTION RATES FOR RECORD

Subscribers make a saving on postage, and receive each *Record* just as soon as it is published. They are also eligible for concessions on newly-published *Ships in Focus* titles. Readers can start their subscription with *any* issue, and are welcome to backdate it to receive previous issues.

	3 issues	6 issues	9 issues
UK	£23	£44	£63
Europe (airmail)	£25	£47	£68
Rest of world (surface mail)	£25	£47	£68
Rest of world (airmail)	£30	£56	£81

John B. Hill's account of Houlder's post-war ships which carried Grange names continues overleaf, with details of each ship and its career, and many more photographs to complete the pictorial survey of this interestingly varied fleet. This is a further view of *Hornby Grange* which was illustrated in part 1. Her details are on page 197. [P. Ransome-Wallis, Roy Fenton collection]

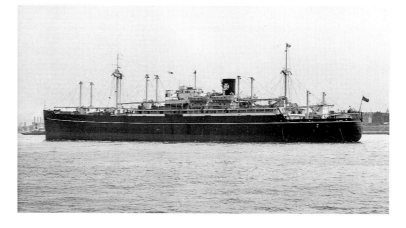

The B26-type bulk carrier *Upwey Grange* of 1976, see ship no. 16. *[Author's collection]*

3. HORNBY GRANGE 1946-1969 Twin-screw refrigerated cargo ship

O.N. 181528 10,785g 6,505n 479.6 x 65.75 x 31.0 feet.
Two Hawthorn-Doxford 4-cyl. 2SCSA oil engines by Hawthorn, Leslie and Co. Ltd., Newcastle-upon-Tyne driving twin screws; 8,900 BHP, 15 knots.
Insulated capacity 555,820 cubic feet.
12 passengers in single berth cabins.
31.5.1946: Launched by Hawthorn, Leslie and Co. Ltd., Hebburn-on-Tyne (Yard No. 683) for Houlder Line Ltd. (Houlder Brothers and Co. Ltd., managers), London as HORNBY GRANGE.
12.12.1946: Delivered.
14.3.1969: Sold to Royal Mail Lines Ltd. (Furness Withy and Co. Ltd., managers), London and renamed DOURO.
1970: Transferred to Prince Line Ltd., London.
6.6.1972: Arrived at Aviles, Spain for demolition.
1.7.1972: Demolition commenced by Desguaces y Salvamentos, Aviles.

4. URMSTON GRANGE 1946-1959 Part-refrigerated cargo ship

O.N.168988 7,051g 4,194n 477.5 x 56.1 x 26.25 feet.
T-3cyl. by Rankin and Blackmore Ltd., Greenock; 10 knots.
Insulated capacity (in numbers 2 and 4 holds) 229,906 cubic feet.
2.9.1942: Launched by Lithgows Ltd., Port Glasgow (Yard No. 980).
11.1942: Completed for the Ministry of War Transport (Houlder Brothers and Co. Ltd., managers), London as EMPIRE PIBROCH.
11.4.1946: Acquired by Houlder Line Ltd. (Houlder Brothers and Co. Ltd., managers), London and renamed URMSTON GRANGE.
2.10.1959: Sold to Argonaut Shipping and Trading Co. (A. Lusi), Piraeus, Greece for £50,000 and renamed ARGO GRANGE.
18.12.1959: Arrived at Hong Kong for demolition.
14.1.1960: Demolition commenced by Leung Yau Trading Co. at Hong Kong.

5. OVINGDEAN GRANGE 1946-1959 Part-refrigerated cargo ship

O.N. 168987 7,046g 4,204n 447.6 x 56.2 x 26.3 feet.
T. 3-cyl. by David Rowan and Co. Ltd., Glasgow; 10.5 knots.
Insulated capacity (in numbers 2 and 4 holds) 229,900 cubic feet. Insulation removed at Hull in February 1952.
30.6.1942: Launched by Lithgows Ltd., Port Glasgow (Yard No. 979).
9.1942: Completed for the Ministry of War Transport, London (Houlder Brothers and Co. Ltd., London, managers) as EMPIRE BUCKLER. Registered at Greenock.
4.5.1946: Acquired by Houlder Line Ltd. (Houlder Brothers and Co. Ltd., managers), London and renamed OVINGDEAN GRANGE.
21.1.1959: Sold to Devon Shipping Co. Ltd., Monrovia, Liberia (Empresa Navegacion Proamar S.R.L. (Renato Ascoli), Buenos Aires, Argentina) for £115,000 and renamed SABRINA.
2.1961: Sold to Cia. Nav. Marcasa, Panama (S. Castell and Co. Ltd., London, managers), renamed NOEMI and registered in Beirut.
27.12.1965: Grounded one mile south west of Ras Abu ar Rasas, on the south western tip of Masirah Island, Oman in position 20.10 north by 58.38 east and abandoned whilst on passage from Matanzas, Cuba to Basrah with a cargo of bagged sugar.
3.1.1966: Declared a constructive total loss.

6. LANGTON GRANGE 1946-1960 Part-refrigerated cargo ship

O.N.168991 7,069g 4,194n 447.5 x 56.2 x 26.25 feet.
T. 3-cyl. by David Rowan and Co. Ltd., Glasgow; 10.5 knots.
Insulated capacity (in numbers 2 and 4 holds) 229,900 cubic feet.
30.9.1942: Launched by Lithgows Ltd., Port Glasgow (Yard No. 972).
12.1942: Completed for the Ministry of War Transport, London (B. and S. Shipping Co. Ltd., Cardiff, managers) as EMPIRE PENNANT. Registered at Greenock.
5.1946: Acquired by Houlder Line Ltd. (Houlder Brothers and Co. Ltd., managers), London and renamed LANGTON GRANGE.
30.5.1960: Sold to H. Sienmin and Sons (Hong Kong) Ltd., Hong Kong for £64,000. Intended to be renamed YESIMA.
5.10.1960: Arrived at Hong Kong for demolition still as LANGTON GRANGE.
26.10.1960: Demolition commenced by Hong Kong Chiap Hua Manufacturing Co. (1947) Ltd.

7. ELSTREE GRANGE 1947-1960 Liberty-type cargo ship

O.N.169783 7,277g 4,453n 422.8 x 56.9 x 27.7 feet.
T. 3-cyl. by General Machinery Corporation, Hamilton, Ontario; 2,500 IHP, 11 knots.

31.12.1943: Launched by Bethlehem-Fairfield Shipyard Inc., Baltimore, Maryland (Yard No. 2304) for the United States War Shipping Administration, New York as SAMETTRICK.

1.1944: Completed and bare-boat chartered to the Ministry of War Transport, London (P. and O. Steam Navigation Co. Ltd., London, managers).

25.4.1947: Acquired by Houlder Line Ltd. (Houlder Brothers and Co. Ltd., managers), London and renamed ELSTREE GRANGE.

24.10.1960: Sold to Centromor Centrala Morska (Polish Ocean Lines), Gdynia, Poland for £106,000 and renamed KOPALNIA MIECHOWICE.

8.1.1972: Rudder post fractured off the Portugese coast whilst on passage from Gdynia to Civitavecchia with coal. Temporary repairs made at Lisbon and cargo delivered.

9.3.1972: Sold via Eurometco Anstalt, Lichtenstein to Brodospas.

25.3.1972: Arrived at Split from Naples for demolition by Brodospas.

10.5.1972: Work complete.

8. BARTON GRANGE 1949-1958 Part-refrigerated cargo ship

O.N. 169514 7,200g 4,946n 447.8 x 56.2 x 26.8 feet.
T. 3-cyl. by Harland and Wolff Ltd., Glasgow, installed by Rankin and Blackmore Ltd., Greenock; 10 knots.
Insulated capacity 285,640 cubic feet. Insulation removed at Newport, Monmouthshire in March 1954.

27.6.1944: Launched by Lithgows Ltd., Port Glasgow (Yard No. 998).

9.1944: Completed for the Ministry of War Transport, London (Elders and Fyffes Ltd., London, managers) as EMPIRE BALFOUR. Registered at Greenock.

1946: Managers became Houlder Brothers and Co. Ltd., London.

7.5.1949: Acquired by Houlder Line Ltd. (Houlder Brothers and Co. Ltd., managers), London and renamed BARTON GRANGE. Registered at Newport, Monmouthshire.

11.7.1958: Sold to Western Steamship Co. Ltd. (Wang Kee and Co. Ltd., Hong Kong) (Wallem and Co. Ltd., Hong Kong, managers) for £116,000; renamed SUNLIGHT and registered at Panama.

6.1962: Sold to the Pan-Nourse Steam Ship Co. S.A., Panama (Wallem and Co. Ltd., managers), Hong Kong.

30.3.1967: Arrived at Hong Kong for demolition by Wise Investment Co. Ltd.

9. ROYSTON GRANGE 1950-1952 Fort type cargo ship

O.N.168470 7,133g 4,245n 441.5 x 57.2 x 27.8 feet.
T. 3-cyl. by Dominion Engine Works, Montreal; 2,500 IHP, 10 knots.

4.3.1943: Launched by the Burrard Drydock Co., North Vancouver, British Columbia (Yard No. 174) for the Canadian Government.

4.1943: Completed and bareboat chartered to the Ministry of War Transport, London (Dene Shipping Co. Ltd., London, managers) as FORT ASH.

4.4.1946: Managers became Houlder Brothers and Co. Ltd., London.

8.1950: Acquired by Houlder Line Ltd. (Houlder Brothers and Co. Ltd., managers), London and renamed ROYSTON GRANGE.

14.10.1952: Sold to I.N.S.A. Societa di Navigazione, Genoa, Italy for £300,000 and renamed GIUAN.

1960: Sold to Compagnia di Navigazione Portoria (Ottavio Novella), Genoa and renamed CINQUETERRE.

1961: Sold to Myrrinella Naviera S.A. (Theo Papadimitriou), Piraeus and renamed TILEMAHOS.

1965: Sold to Triton Shipping (Gibraltar) Ltd., Gibraltar (G.E. Houry and Son Ltd., London) and renamed ELICOS.

28.1.1966: Aground.

6.2.1966: Refloated but later sold for demolition.

12.7.1966: Arrived in tow at Split for demolition by Brodospas. Price paid £45,000.

10. OSWESTRY GRANGE 1952-1971

O.N.184610 9,405g 5,516n 475.0 x 61.6 x 29.7 feet.
Hawthorn-Doxford type 4-cyl. 2SCSA oil engine by Hawthorn, Leslie and Co. Ltd., Newcastle-upon-Tyne; 3,780 BHP, 12.5 knots.
4 passengers.

3.10.1951: Launched by Hawthorn, Leslie and Co. Ltd., Hebburn-on-Tyne (Yard No. 708) for Houlder Line Ltd. (Houlder Brothers and Co. Ltd., managers), London as OSWESTRY GRANGE.

17.4.1952: Completed at a cost of £601,318.

20.2.1971: Sold to Glyfada Seafaring Corporation, Panama (Methenitis Brothers, Piraeus, Greece) for £150,000 and renamed DINOS METHENITIS under the Greek flag

28.7.1977: Laid up at Chalkis.

1978: Sold to Seafreight Holding Corporation, Panama for $300,000 and renamed DINOS V.

1.1.1979: Beached at Gadani for demolition by Haydari Shipbreaking Industries (Al-Murtasa Metal and Steel Co.).

Opposite upper: The only Liberty to carry a Grange name, *Elstree Grange.* [A Duncan, author's collection]

Opposite lower: *Barton Grange.* In a departure from Houlder's usual colours, her name is painted in black on the white forecastle. *[Fotoflite incorporating Skyfotos, author's collection]*

This page above: The 'Fort' type *Royston Grange* with the more usual black forecastle. *[J. and M. Clarkson]*

Right: *Oswestry Grange* with a deck cargo of buses. *[Author's collection]*

Above: *Thorpe Grange* and, below left, during her 14 months running as *St. Merriel*. [Above: Fotoflite incorporating Skyfotos, author's collection; below J. and M. Clarkson]

Below: *Denby Grange* and, above right, following her conversion to a parcels tanker and renaming *Stolt Grange*. [Below: F.W. Hawks, G.R. Scott collection; above A. Duncan, author's collection]

200

11. THORPE GRANGE 1954-1972

O.N. 186044 8,694g 5,120n 476.9 x 62.0 x 29.8 feet.
Wallsend-Doxford type 4-cyl. 2SCSA oil engine by Wallsend Slipway and Engineering Co. Ltd., Wallsend-on-Tyne; 4,400 BHP, 13.25 knots.
8.12.1953: Launched by Bartram and Sons Ltd., Sunderland (Yard No. 343) for Houlder Line Ltd. (Houlder Brothers and Co. Ltd., managers), London as THORPE GRANGE.
27.4.1954: Completed at a cost of £653,160.
1966: Owners became the South American Saint Line Ltd. (Houlder Brothers and Co. Ltd., managers), London and renamed ST. MERRIEL.
1971: Owners became Houlder Line Ltd. (Houlder Brothers and Co. Ltd., managers), London and renamed THORPE GRANGE.
24.10.1971: Laid up at Falmouth because of seamen's strike.
8.1972: Owners became the South American Saint Line Ltd. (Houlder Brothers and Co. Ltd., managers), London and renamed ST. MERRIEL.
10.1973: Sold to Joo Hong Maritime Navigation Pte. Ltd. (Ngoh Hong Hang (Pte.), managers), Singapore and renamed JOO HONG.
1975: Sold to Li-Ta Shipping Co. (Pte.) Inc., Singapore and renamed PAN TECK.
1977: Renamed LIVA and registered in Malaysia.
25.3.1977: Arrived at Colombo.
2.1978: Broke moorings and in collision whilst under arrest at Colombo.
1978: Reported to have been sold and to be renamed SELAMAT SINDIA.
2.1979: Sold to Taiwan shipbreakers for $124 per light deadweight ton.
10.3.1979: Sailed from Colombo in charge of the Dutch motor tug ORINOCO (670/1964).
4.4.1979: Arrived at Kaohsiung for demolition.

12. DENBY GRANGE 1958-1969 Tanker

O.N. 187822 12,391g 7,169n 559.3 x 72.2 x 29.6 feet.
Steam turbine by Hawthorn, Leslie (Engineers) Ltd., Newcastle-upon-Tyne; 8,250 SHP, 14.5 knots.
2.4.1958: Launched by Hawthorn, Leslie (Shipbuilders) Ltd., Hebburn-on-Tyne (Yard No. 735) for Houlder Line Ltd. (Houlder Brothers and Co. Ltd., managers), London as DENBY GRANGE.
22.7.1958: Delivered at a cost of £1,475,287.
1968: Converted into parcels/chemical tanker by Kristiansands M/V, Kristiansand and renamed STOLT GRANGE.
5.2.1969: Commenced five-year charter to Jakob Stolt-Nielsen, Haugesund, Norway.
18.5.1973: Sold to the Dundee Shipping Inc., Monrovia (Jakob Stolt-Nielsen, Haugesund, Norway) together with STOLT STUART, STOLT TUDOR and STOLT ABADESA for $2,500,000 million and renamed STOLT PUMA.
1976: Owners became Nord Shipping Inc., Monrovia (Stolt-Nielsens Rederi A/S, Haugesund) and renamed PUMA.
16.9.1976: Arrived at Kaohsiung for demolition by Li Chong Steel and Iron Works Ltd.

13. ROYSTON GRANGE 1959-1972 Refrigerated cargo ship

O.N. 301035 9,035g 5,027n 489.0 x 65.6 x 29.0 feet.
Steam turbine by Hawthorn, Leslie (Engineers) Ltd., Newcastle-upon-Tyne; 8,500 SHP, 16 knots.
Insulated capacity 464,670 cubic feet.
12 passengers in 6 single and 3 double berth cabins.
23.6.1959: Launched by Hawthorn, Leslie (Shipbuilders) Ltd, Hebburn-on-Tyne (Yard No. 736) for Houlder Line Ltd. (Houlder Brothers and Co. Ltd., managers), London as ROYSTON GRANGE.
15.12.1959: Delivered at a cost of £2,380,000.
11.5.1972: In collision with the Liberian tanker TIEN CHEE (12,595/1955) in Indio Channel, River Plate, whilst on passage from Buenos Aires to Montevideo. ROYSTON GRANGE caught fire, and her entire crew of 61 plus three relatives, ten passengers and the Argentine pilot lost their lives.
27.5.1972: Towed to Montevideo, declared a constructive total loss, and cargo discharged.
23.6.1972: Laid up pending outcome of legal arguments regarding ownership and salvage claims.
27.3.1974: Left Montevideo in tow of the German motor tug HANSA (383/1967).
20.5.1974: Arrived Barcelona and demolished six months later by Desguaces Cataluna S.A.

The ill-fated *Royston Grange.* [Author's collection]

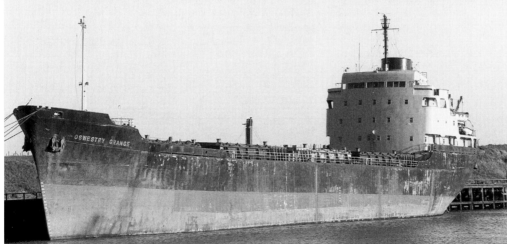

Above: *Hardwicke Grange.* *[J. and M. Clarkson]*

Left: the collier *Oswestry Grange* waiting to load at Blyth in November 1984. Masts and superstructure are painted light green, and her hull paint looks distinctly worn. *[Author's collection]*

14. HARDWICKE GRANGE 1961-1977 Refrigerated cargo ship

O.N. 302613 9,234g 5,086n 489.0 x 65.8 x 29.0 feet.
Steam turbine by Hawthorn, Leslie (Engineers) Ltd., Newcastle-upon-Tyne; 8,500 SHP, 16 knots.
Insulated capacity 464,670 cubic feet.
12 passengers in six single and three double berth cabins.
21.9.1960: Launched by Hawthorn, Leslie (Shipbuilders) Ltd., Hebburn-on-Tyne for Houlder Line Ltd. (Houlder Brothers and Co. Ltd., managers), London as HARDWICKE GRANGE.
20.3.1961: Delivered.
17.6.1977: Sold to Montezillion Navigation Corporation, Monrovia (F. De Perrot, Neuchâtel, Switzerland) and renamed JACQUES.
27.3.1979: Arrived at Kaohsiung having been sold to breakers for $911,155.
14.5.1979: Breaking up began by Shyeh Sheng Huat Steel and Iron, Kaohsiung.

15. OSWESTRY GRANGE 1974-1985 Bulk-carrier/collier

O.N. 306163 5,617g 2,725n 369.9 x 53.5 x 25.5 feet.
Stork-Werkspoor type 6-cyl. 2SCSA oil engine by N.V.

Werkspoor, Amsterdam, installed by George Clark Ltd., Sunderland; 4,500 BHP, 13.5 knots.
10.6.1964: Launched by Bartram and Sons, Sunderland (Yard No. 399) for Wm. France, Fenwick and Co. Ltd., London as CHELWOOD.
11.1964: Delivered.
1972: Managers became Houlder Brothers and Co. Ltd., London.
1974: Acquired by Houlder Brothers and Co. Ltd., London and renamed OSWESTRY GRANGE.
1984: Owners became Stevinson, Hardy (Tankers) Ltd. (Houlder Brothers and Co. Ltd., managers), London.
5.8.1985: Sold to Oxelosund Hamn A/B, Oxelosund, Sweden and renamed STENJOHAN for use as a static coal distribution centre in the Oxelosund district.
1990: In use by Lucky Marine Enterprise S.A. (Dido Shipping Co., managers), St. Vincent as a trans-shipment barge.
1994: Sold to Tamara Shipping Ltd., San Lorenzo, Honduras and renamed GINA T.
1995: In use by Tarbin Maritime Ltd., Limassol as a general cargo barge, renamed EL BILLY and then GINA T, latterly under the Syrian flag.
9.11.2001: Reported laid up at Beirut.

16. UPWEY GRANGE 1976-1982 B26 type bulk carrier

O.N. 366139 15,903g 11,082n 183.0 x 22.8 x 10.47 metres
Clark North Eastern Marine-Sulzer type 6-cyl. oil engine by George Clark and North Eastern Marine Engineering Ltd., Wallsend-on-Tyne; 9,900 BHP, 15 knots.

3.3.1976: Launched by Austin and Pickersgill Ltd., Southwick, Sunderland (Yard No. 902) for Alexander Shipping Co. Ltd. (Houlder Brothers and Co. Ltd., managers), London as UPWEY GRANGE. She was originally to have been named AYLESBURY.

21.7.1976: Delivered.

1982: Sold to Ace Pacific Navigation Co., Panama (Fuyo Sogo Lease K.K., Tokyo, Japan), and renamed LILY VILLAGE.

1987: Sold to Carton Overseas Inc., Panama (Seama International Shipping), Panama for $1,600,000 and renamed PUGGI.

1990: Sold to Congress Shipping Co. Ltd. (Transcontinental Maritime and Trading S.A., Piraeus), renamed NATALIA and registered at Limassol.

1991: Owners became Observer Shipping Co. Ltd., Limassol (Transcontinental Maritime and Trading S.A., Piraeus) and renamed RANGER.

1995: Sold to Orgullo Navigation Ltd., Panama (Allied Maritime Inc., Athens), and renamed ORGULLO.

11.2001: Still in service.

17. LYNTON GRANGE 1976-1982 B 26 type bulk carrier

O.N. 366279 15,903g 11,082n 183.04 x 22.76 x 10.478 metres.

Hawthorn-Sulzer type 6-cyl. 2SCSA oil engine by Hawthorn, Leslie (Engineers) Ltd., Newcastle-upon-Tyne; 9,900 BHP, 15 knots.

12.5.1976: Launched by Austin and Pickersgill Ltd., Southwick, Sunderland (Yard No. 903) for Alexander Shipping Co. Ltd. (Houlder Brothers and Co. Ltd., managers), London as LYNTON GRANGE.

1.9.1976: Delivered.

1982: Sold to Central Shipping (Holdings) Inc., Panama (Fuyo Sogo Lease K.K., Tokyo, Japan) and renamed NORTHERN CHERRY.

1990: Sold to Chios Charm Shipping Co. S.A., Panama (Harbor Shipping and Trading S.A., Chios, Greece) and renamed CHIOS CHARM.

15.9.2000: Damaged when came into contact with Cote St. Catherines Lock on the St. Lawrence Seaway whilst on a voyage from Puerto Cabello to Windsor, Ontario in ballast.

16.12.2000: Arrived at Alang to be broken up.

Left: a photograph taken by the master of *Upwey Grange,* Capain Wilcox, of her deck cargo of timber loaded in the Far East and bound for Rotterdam and Liverpool. *[Author's collection]*

Below: *Lynton Grange,* sister to *Upwey Grange. [Author's collection]*

18. DUNSTER GRANGE 1977-1982 Bulk carrier.
O.N. 334651 24,023g 16,863n 666.0 x 92.2 x 38.1 feet.
Scott-Sulzer type 6-cyl. 2SCSA oil engine by Scott's Shipbuilding and Engineering Co. Ltd., Greenock; 13,611 BHP, 15 knots.
7.3.1967: Launched by Scott's Shipbuilding and Engineering Co. Ltd., Greenock (Yard No. 707) for the Hadley Shipping Co. Ltd., Houlder Line Ltd. and Empire Transport Co. Ltd. (Warwick and Esplen Ltd., managers), London as CLYDESDALE.
1969: Time chartered to Seabridge Shipping Co. and renamed CLYDE BRIDGE.
1974: Owners became Houlder Brothers and Co. Ltd., London (Warwick and Esplen Ltd., managers).

1.1977: Renamed DUNSTER GRANGE (Houlder Brothers, Bulk Shipping Division, managers), London.
2.1981: Owners became Stevinson, Hardy (Tankers) Ltd. (Houlder Brothers and Co. Ltd., managers), London.
3.1982: Sold to Gulf Shipping Lines Ltd. (Gokal Brothers, Gulfeast Shipmanagement Ltd., Hong Kong) and renamed GULF KESTREL. Houlder Brothers and Co. Ltd. remained managers until 3.1983.
3.1983: Transferred to Graphite Shipping Inc., Monrovia (Gulfeast Shipmanagement Ltd., Hong Kong, managers) and renamed FIVE STAR.
31.8.1986: Arrived at Kaohsiung for demolition by Nan Engineering Steel Co.

Above: *Dunster Grange. [A. Duncan, G.R. Scott collection]*

Below: Houlder's bulk carrier *Orotava* which ran briefly as *Ripon Grange. [Fotoflite incorporating Skyfotos]*

19. RIPON GRANGE 1979-1980 Bulk carrier.

O.N. 334768 28,880g 20,614n 716.3 x 92.3 x 41.2 feet.
Doxford type 6-cyl. 2SCSA oil engine by Doxford and
Sunderland Shipbuilding and Engineering Co. Ltd.,
Sunderland; 13,500 BHP, 15.5 knots.
3.11.1967: Launched by Doxford and Sunderland
Shipbuilding and Engineering Co. Ltd., Sunderland (Yard
No. 842) for Ore Carriers Ltd. (Houlder Brothers and Co.
Ltd., managers), London as OROTAVA.
2.1968: Completed at a cost of £2,145,525.
1969: Time chartered by Seabridge Shipping Co. and
renamed OROTAVA BRIDGE (Houlder Brothers and Co.
Ltd., managers), London.
1974: Renamed OROTAVA at end of charter.
1978: Owners became Alexander Shipping Co. Ltd.
(Houlder Brothers and Co. Ltd., managers), London.
1979: Owners became Furness, Withy and Co. Ltd.
(Houlder Brothers and Co. Ltd., managers), London and
renamed RIPON GRANGE.
1980: Sold to Leda Segundo Compañia Naviera S.A.,
Panama (S. Stravelakis, Piraeus) and renamed LEDA.
1982: Owners became Unity Enterprises Co., Valletta,
Malta (S. Stravelakis, Piraeus) and renamed UNITY.
1984: Owners became Romneya Shipping Corporation,
Monrovia (S. Stravelakis, Piraeus), renamed LATINI and
registered in Piraeus.
3.1986: Sold to Chinese shipbreakers and arrived at
Huangpu, Guangdong Province from Tricomalee about
25.4.1986.

20. HORNBY GRANGE 1979-1984 Oil tanker

O.N. 379972 39,6269 25,730n 228.28 x 32.26 x 13.3
metres.
Burmeister & Wain type 6-cyl. 2SCSA oil engine by
Harland and Wolff Ltd., Belfast; 20,500 BHP, 16 knots.
5.10.1978: Launched by Harland and Wolff Ltd., Belfast
(Yard No. 1709) for the Alexander Shipping Co. Ltd.
(Houlder Brothers and Co. Ltd., managers), London as
HORNBY GRANGE.
6.1979: Completed.

1984: Ownership transferred to Shaw, Savill and Albion Co.
Ltd. (Houlder Brothers and Co. Ltd., managers), London.
14.12.1984: Transferred to Fest Atlantic Co. Ltd. (Far East
Transport Co.) (Island Navigation Co., C.Y. Tung, Hong
Kong, managers), Monrovia and renamed SANTA
BARBARA.
1987: Managers became Denholm Ship Management
(Overseas) Ltd.
6.1989: Sold to Transpetrol Navigation Pty. Ltd., Singapore
(Transpetrol Services N.V., Brussels, Belgium) (Wallem
Ltd., London, managers) for $13,500,000 and renamed
AFFINITY.
18.5.2000: Arrived at Alang for demolition having been
sold to Mahendra Steel Traders, Alang for $2,060,000.
21.5.2000: Work began.

21. ELSTREE GRANGE 1979-1985 Oil tanker

O.N. 388166 39,626g 25,730n 228.25 x 32.31 x 13.301
metres.
Burmeister & Wain type 6-cyl. 2SCSA oil engine by
Harland and Wolff Ltd., Belfast; 20,500 BHP, 15.5 knots.
26.1.1979: Launched by Harland and Wolff Ltd., Belfast
(Yard No. 1710) for the Alexander Shipping Co. Ltd.
(Houlder Brothers and Co. Ltd., managers), London as
ELSTREE GRANGE.
10.1979: Completed.
1984: Owners became Shaw, Savill and Albion Co. Ltd.
(Houlder Brothers and Co. Ltd., managers), London.
1985: Transferred to Fest Pacific Co. Ltd. (Far East
Transport Co.) (Island Navigation Co., C.Y. Tung, Hong
Kong, managers), Monrovia and renamed SANTA LUCIA.
1987: Managers became Denholm Shipmanagement
(Overseas) Ltd.
6.1989: Sold to White Tankers Private Ltd., Singapore
(Transpetrol Services N.V., Brussels), (Wallem Ltd.,
London, managers) for $13,500,000 and renamed SPIRIT.
28.4.2000: Arrived at Alang for demolition by Crown Steel
Company, Alang, having been sold for $2,060,000.
9.5.2000: Work began.

Hornby Grange. [Author's collection]

22. ROUNTON GRANGE 1980-1984 Bulk carrier

O.N. 376924. 40,753g 27,867n 244.1 x 32.29 x 12.917 metres.
3 Maj-Sulzer type 6-cyl. 2SCSA oil engine by Tvornica Dizel Motora '3 Maj', Rijeka, Yugoslavia; 17,400 BHP, 15.5 knots.
19.12.1971: Launched by Brodogradiliste '3 Maj', Rijeka (Yard No. 543) for Salenrederierna (Rederi A/B Disa), Stockholm as PACIFIC WASA.
4.1972: Delivered.
1978: Ownership transferred to Mainquill Ltd., Bristol (Spanocean Line Ltd., London, a company associated with Salenrederierna).
1980: Sold to Furness, Withy and Co. Ltd. (Houlder Brothers and Co. Ltd., managers), London and renamed ROUNTON GRANGE. Registered at Bristol.
8.10.1982-5.1983: Laid up at Glasgow.
1984: Sold to Highly Enterprise Corporation, Keelung, Taiwan (Chong Shing Ocean Enterprise Corporation, Taipei) and renamed CHINA MARQUIS.
4.1986: Sold to Nan Tai Line Co., Taipei and renamed OCEAN PEACE.
10.1988: Sold to Penta Navigation Co. Ltd., Monrovia (Forum Maritime S.A., Piraeus) for $6,650,000 and renamed FORUM GLORY under the Greek flag.
1994: Owners became Mainprize Shipping Co. Ltd., Limassol, Cyprus (Forum Maritime S.A., Piraeus).
1997: Sold to Albany Maritime Ltd., St. Vincent and renamed SUN GLORY.
1997: Sold to Katona Investment Co. (Dalex Shipping Co. S.A., managers), St. Vincent and renamed MONTREUX.
16.3.1998: Arrived at Alang for demolition by the Virat Shipbreaking Corporation, Alang who began work that day.

23. BEACON GRANGE 1982-1984

O.N. 360122 12,321g 6,798n 161.45 x 22.36 x 8.637 metres.
Burmeister & Wain type 8-cyl. 2SCSA oil engine by J.G.Kincaid and Co. Ltd., Greenock; 15,000 BHP, 18 knots.
21.12.1972: Launched by Cammell Laird and Co. Ltd, Birkenhead (Yard No. 1355) for the Pacific Steam Navigation Co. Ltd., Liverpool as ORDUNA.
3.1973: Delivered.
30.9.1982: Transferred to Royal Mail Lines Ltd. (Furness, Withy (Shipping) Ltd., managers), London and renamed BEACON GRANGE. Outward voyages were on charter to Cenargo Ltd.
8.1984: Sold to Cenargo Ltd. (Denholm (Bermuda) Ltd. managers), Hamilton, Bermuda and renamed MERCHANT PIONEER.
8.1993: Sold to Jennyship S.A. (Great Circle Shippng Agency Ltd., Bangkok, managers) for $2,200,000, renamed JENNIFER R and registered in Panama.
9.1997: Sold to Saiful Islam and Brothers, Chittagong, Bangladesh for demolition.
16.9.1997: Arrived at Chittagong where work began the next day.

Rounton Grange in January 1983.

Origins of the 'Grange' names

The use of the suffix 'Grange' can be traced back to 1878, when the founder, Edwin Savory Houlder, moved into a new family home, 'The Grange', at Sutton, Surrey. The first adopted was *Hornby Grange,* used in 1890, and it became the custom to display a picture of the house after which the ship was named on stairways leading to the passengers' dining saloons.

In the early days permission to use the names was always sought from the owners of the properties, but this custom lapsed as some of the original houses were sold or demolished. One tradition which was maintained was using only names which began with one of the letters of 'Houlder Brothers.'

As far as possible, using company archives, the origin of the 'Grange' names is given below. As some of them were adopted upwards of one hundred years ago, the houses may no longer exist and it has not always been possible to establish their precise location.

Name	Location	Home of
Barton Grange	Pitminster near Taunton, Devon	The Newton family
Beacon Grange	Near Wrexham, North Wales	Admiral Waddelove
Denby Grange	Near Dewsbury, West Yorkshire	Sir John Lister Kaye
Dunster Grange	Dunster, Somerset	
Elstree Grange	Probably Elstree, Hertfordshire	
Hardwicke Grange	Shrewsbury	R.H. Sipson, and formerly Frank Bibby of Bibby Line
Hornby Grange	Near Northallerton, North Yorkshire	Mr. Horsefall
Langton Grange	Spilsby, Lincolnshire	The Trotter family
Lynton Grange	Probably Lynton, Devon	
Oswestry Grange	Probably Oswestry, Shropshire	
Ovingdean Grange	Near Brighton, Sussex	
Ripon Grange	Probably Ripon, North Yorkshire	
Rippingham Grange	Little Weighton, near Hull	F. Nottingham
Royston Grange	Probably Royston, Cambridgeshire	
Rounton Grange	Northallerton, North Yorkshire	Major Maurice Lowthian Bell
Thorpe Grange	Aldmondbury, near Huddersfield, West Yorkshire	The venerable R.C.M. Harvey, Archdeacon of Halifax
Upwey Grange	Upwey, near Dorchester, Dorset	
Urmston Grange	Probably Urmston, near Manchester	

Furness Canada Ltd., Montreal

Desirous of re-opening a cargo service between Canadian ports and the east coast of South America, Furness, Withy were obliged to comply with Canadian Government requirements to employ ships registered in Canada and manned by Canadians. For this reason a new company was formed in Montreal in 1947, jointly between Furness, Withy, Prince Line and Houlder Brothers and Co. Ltd., London. The new venture - Furness (Canada) Ltd., Montreal - purchased four Park-type ships, two of which were renamed *Beacon Grange* and *Royston Grange* (the other two were the *Brazilian Prince* (ex *Outremont Park*) and *Royal Prince* (ex *Elgin Park*), which clearly reflected the involvement of Houlder Brothers and the Prince Line in the enterprise. Unfortunately, the new business was short-lived, but details of the two 'Grange' ships involved appear below.

BEACON GRANGE 1948-1949
O.N. 176014 7,157g 4,284n 441.5 x 57.2 x 27. 7 feet.
T. 3-cyl. by Dominion Engineering Works Ltd., Montreal; 2,500 IHP, 11 knots.
14.2.1945: Launched by Burrard Drydock Co. Ltd., Vancouver, British Columbia (Yard No. 231) for the Park Steamship Co. Ltd., Montreal as ALBERT PARK.
11.4.1945: Delivered.
1946: Transferred the Canadian Transport Co. Ltd.,

Montreal and renamed HARMAC VICTORIA.
1948: Sold to Furness (Canada) Ltd., Montreal and renamed BEACON GRANGE.
1949: Sold to Conquistadora Cia. Nav., Panama and renamed CONSTANTINOS
19.3.1967: Left Hong Kong to be broken up in China.
31.7.1967: Delivered to shipbreakers at Shanghai and demolished during August 1967.

ROYSTON GRANGE 1948-1949.
O.N. 175355 7,166g 4,317n 411.5 x 57.2 x 27.7 feet.
T-3cyl. by Dominion Engineering Works Ltd., Montreal; 2,500 IHP, 11 knots.
20.10.1943: Launched by Burrard Drydock Co. Ltd., Vancouver, British Columbia (Yard No. 195) for the Ministry of War Transport, London as FORT TOULOUSE, but transfer to UK cancelled.
1.1.1944: Delivered to the Park Steamship Co. Ltd., Montreal as SAPPERTON PARK.
1946: Transferred to the Canadian Transport Co. Ltd., Montreal and renamed HARMAC ALBERNI.
1948: Acquired by Furness (Canada) Ltd., Montreal and renamed ROYSTON GRANGE.
1949: Sold to Compañia Prospero S.A. (Rio Pardo Compañia S.A. Goulandris Brothers, managers) and renamed YIANNIS.
12.12.1966: Arrived at Mihara, Japan for demolition.

The two Furness (Canada) granges: *Beacon Grange* (above) and *Royston Grange* (below) at Montevideo on 14th June 1948. *[Above: G.R. Scott collection; below: Raul Maya, W.A. Schell collection]*

THE NILE STEAMSHIP CO. LTD.
David Burrell

Since 1966 observers have noted the Nile Steamship Co. Ltd. as owners of ships under various managements. They recalled a company of the same name, managed by Glen and Co., Glasgow. Was there a connection?

Lithgow ownership

The Nile Steamship Co. Ltd. was registered in Edinburgh on 18th November 1919 (Company No. 10756). All 5,000 £10 shares were controlled by shipbuilders James Lithgow (1883-1952) and his brother Henry (1886-1948). It was formed to own yard number 715, a Lithgow standard design built on speculation and launched on 1st October 1919 as *Nile*.

Nile cost £210,000, paid for by shares and bills for £160,000. The story of the company is that of many formed in the heady days during and shortly after the First World War. Voyage profits in 1920 were £101,341. Freight markets collapsed that year and the 1921 profit was £19,446. Subsequent years were worse; 1923 showed a loss of £1,977. The improved market from 1926 to 1928 saw annual profits of about £5,000. A sale could not recover the investment and, over-capitalised, Nile Steamship Co. Ltd. could not service debt, provide for depreciation and pay a dividend.

Laid up at Leith in May 1930, *Nile* was sold for £11,500 in November 1933 to the Brynymor Steam Ship Co. Ltd., Swansea. This company was managed by Ambrose, Davies and Matthews Ltd. who were associated with Jugoslavenska Plovidba D.D., to whom she passed a month later to become the Yugoslav *Sokol*. A magnificent crop of wheat grew on her deck whilst laid up! Becoming the *Rio Grande* in 1939, she came under the control of the Ministry of Shipping in 1940. As *Empire Blanda* she was torpedoed in February 1941.

The sale left Nile insolvent, with no assets and debts of £116,500 (capital £50,000, bills £66,500). Winding up was the usual fate, but Lithgows left Nile dormant until they reactivated it in 1951. The outstanding bills were cancelled and there was a £50,000 recoverable tax loss. Two ships, *Coulbeg* and *Dornoch,* were transferred from Dornoch Shipping for £145,000 and £111,000, respectively. This transaction led to a dispute with the Inland Revenue which was decided in favour of Nile in 1960. The Tax Inspector asserted that as both companies had common beneficial ownership tax should be levied on market values (£270,000 and £300,000) rather than on prices paid. The extra tax demand was for £157,712. The appeal to the Tax Commissioners was upheld as the sale had been arranged by the directors without reference to shareholders. Two senior QCs opinioned that the case was unwinnable, but Junior Counsel James Mackay took the opposite view and carried the day. Mackay had a long association with Lithgows, being created Baron Mackay of Clashfern in 1979 and Lord High Chancellor of Great Britain in 1987. The change in Nile's fortunes also caught the eye of the Examiner of the Court at the Probate Office, who wanted an explanation. He saw outstanding bills gratuitously discharged, new bills issued and large profits (£49,517 in the first year). Had the estate lost £66,500 as a result? Common ownership, albeit through different channels, had to be explained.

Dornoch of Dornoch Shipping Co. Ltd. on trials in the Clyde and wearing the colours of managers Lambert Brothers. *[Glasgow University Archives GD320/10/1/118]*

Dornoch briefly became *Dunrobin* in 1956, and she is seen at Dublin in the colours of Harrisons (Clyde) Ltd. *[R.J. Scott, courtesy of Ivor Rooke]*

Nile reborn

The ships, renamed *Jutland* and *Dunrobin,* came from the Dornoch Shipping Co. Ltd. (company number 17998: formed 1934), managed by Lambert Brothers Ltd., London. Dornoch was owned by Lithgows Ltd. and traded 'spec' ships awaiting buyers and vessels with prototype features. Between 1930 and 1936 Lithgows built five vessels on spec to provide work for the yard, and 39 from 1920 to 1940. In 1953 management of Dornoch was transferred to Glen and Co. Ltd., and, in 1956, the Nile and Dornoch companies passed to Harrisons (Clyde) Ltd. These management changes came about as Lambert Brothers were going through a 'tired' period and Sir William Lithgow's cousin Iain Harrison was entering shipping. Gow, Harrison and Co. had been wound up, so he joined Glen and Co. before opening his own office as Harrisons (Clyde) Ltd.

Employment was typical: a mix of time and voyage charters carrying cargo such as grain, coal, phosphate, sugar, ore and timber. The buoyant market created by post-war rebuilding was extended by the Korean War (1950-1953) and saw the sale of *Jutland* in March 1953 to a Tsavliris company for £385,000. Still under Tsavliris control she foundered in June 1967. The Suez Crisis in 1956 boosted freights but, with the reopening of the canal, they fell off during 1957. *Dunrobin* was kept until 1959 when, as *Vennachar,* she went to Japanese breakers. She had been trading at a loss and realised only £55,000. Although owning no ship, in 1960 Nile had assets of over £360,000, most loaned to Dornoch.

Various proposals were considered in the 1950s. One in 1954 was to merge Nile and Dornoch, Nile either buying Dornoch or just the assets, with Nile's capital to become £300,000 for the purpose. Another proposal was to form a company in Bermuda or the Bahamas. Britain's tax regime meant a British fleet could develop at only half the rate of one owned offshore. The proposal in 1956-7 was that Nile (Atlantic) Ltd. would be a Nile subsidiary and borrow from Dornoch. Starting with a second-hand ship, orders would be placed with Lithgows for tankers and ore carriers. An 18,000dwt tanker for 1964 delivery was proposed, and BISC (Ore) Ltd. were chartering ore carriers built back-to-back with charters. Finally, in February 1964, a charter was signed with Erling Naess' Anglo-Norness Group for a 63,850 tons deadweight bulker. Laid down as Lithgows'

yard number 1157, she was launched as *Naess Talisman* in August 1966.

ICFC ownership

In March 1964 Nile was sold to the Industrial and Commercial Finance Corporation Ltd. (ICFC) (company number 397156, formed 1945) and thereafter acted as owners of ships demise chartered to various operators. Companies also used by ICFC in this role were Ship Mortgage Finance Co. Ltd. (company number 493234: formed 1951) and Falkland Shipowners Ltd. (company number 236018: formed 1928) which was renamed Finance for Shipping Ltd. in 1975 and dissolved in 1996. ICFC had been formed by the Bank of England and the Clearing Banks as a finance vehicle and had interests in a wide range of markets. Ship Mortgage Finance stemmed from proposals by Lithgows and the Anglo-Iranian Oil Co. Ltd. (later British Petroleum) to finance independent tankers. Falkland Shipowners started as the British arm of Norwegian whaling interests Bruun & von der Lippe, owning the factory ship *Anglo-Norse* (7,957/1914) and a fleet of catchers.

In 1961 Lithgows and Fairfields formed Kingston Financial Services (Clyde) Ltd. (KFS) to encourage orders, with Fairfield's Sir John Erskine designated chairman. It appeared to Bill Hay, KFS' company secretary designate, that it was necessary to register under the Moneylenders Acts of 1900 and 1927, or apply to the Board of Trade for exemption. This horrified Sir John: these acts had been drafted to control usury. No self-respecting city businessman wished to be associated with them. The chairman of ICFC, Lord Pearce, was asked how they avoided registering Ship Mortgage Finance. He was likewise stunned, especially when legal counsel confirmed that ICFC were in breach of the law - all loans made were illegal and security held void and unenforceable! A borrower on the verge of defaulting threatened to make the situation public, so was purchased by ICFC. The Ship Mortgage Finance Company Act, 1962 was hastily passed to validate loans and securities of £6.5 million. The Moneylenders Acts themselves were replaced by the Consumer Credit Act, 1974.

At the same time James E. 'Teddy' Boyd, a chartered accountant and director of the Lithgow Group, was developing ideas which led to the sale of Nile to ICFC in 1964. Rather than making loans secured by mortgages, his idea was to build and retain ownership, demise chartering. Generous investment tax allowances accrued (at one stage reaching 140% on British-built and owned ships) and the application of group relief sheltered profits from other sources. It might also benefit charterers as savings could be used to offer better charter rates. But it was necessary to qualify under the tax rules, hence the acquisition of Nile and Falklands, as both qualified with a history of shipowning and continued trading. Finance of a ship for Anglo-Norness saw the idea applied. Pending delivery Nile, for tax purposes, converted to an investment company. The new owners (ICFC had a controlling interest) increased the capital to £1 million in 1964, and £2.3 million in 1966.

By the time *Naess Talisman* was delivered Naess had, with P&O, formed Associated Bulk Carriers Ltd., to whom she was chartered until 1984, with technical management by Denholm Ship Management Ltd. She was only retained until 1978 when she passed to Taiwan interests. As *Panamax Centaurus* she was broken up in 1985 after fire damage.

A wide variety of ships were owned by Nile in its new role, ranging from the grab crane/dredger *W.G. Packman*, the tug *Hector Read* and hydrofoil *Condor 3* to the obo *Tyne Bridge* of 169,000dwt, a sister of the ill-fated *Derbyshire* lost in typhoon 'Orchid' in September 1980. Others were tankers, gas carriers and general cargo ships. In March 1975 the balance sheet recorded the sum invested in ships in excess of £45 million. The fleet since 1966 is listed in the accompanying table, and a selection of photographs is included.

In 1985 Nile ceased trading, *Bromley* and *Faraday* being transferred to the parent company. ICFC had been renamed Investors in Industry plc in 1983 and, in 1988, became 3i plc. It has continued as owners, demise chartering a varied fleet, from cruise ships through an array of bulkers, reefers and tankers to tugs, offshore supply ships and barges. Nile remained dormant until dissolved on 19th January 1999.

Name	Built	Gross	Charterer	Year sold
Hector Read	1965	65	Great Yarmouth Port and Haven.	
Orcoma	1966	10,509	Pacific S.N. Co.	1979
Teviot	1966	694	George Gibson and Co.	1978
Clerk-Maxwell	1966	8,298	Houlder Bros. and Co.	1983
Naess Talisman	1967	40,919	Associated Bulk Carriers.	1978
Iron Endeavour	1969	40,316	Dampier Mining Co. (BHP).	1983
Manchester Concorde	1969	11,899	Manchester Liners.	1982
Silverhawk	1969	6,771	Silver Line.	1983
Baknes	1970	13,241	H. Clarkson and Co./Jebsens.	1978
Faraday	1971	19,754	Houlder Bros. & Co.	1984*
Manchester Crusade	1971	12,042	Manchester Liners.	1982
Condor 3	1971	129	O. Dorey and Sons.	1979
Tyne Bridge	1972	91,100	Hunting and Sons.	1979
Bernes	1972	22,901	J. and J. Denholm/Jebsens.	1980
Joseph R. Smallwood	1972	19,869	Common Bros.	1980
W.G. Packman	1972	649	M.B. Dredging.	
Frank D. Moores	1973	19,869	Common Bros.	1980
Bromley	1978	640	Bowker and King.	1985*

*Transferred to Investors in Industry plc

Naess Talisman. [Fotoflite incorporating Skyfotos]

The first of the wide variety of ships owned by Nile Steamship Co. Ltd. under its new guise as a finance company was the tug *Hector Read,* operated by Great Yarmouth Port and Haven. *[J. and M. Clarkson]*

Nile's ships came from a number of different yards. The motorship *Orcoma* was built and engined by Harland and Wolff Ltd. for charter to Pacific Steam Navigation Company, which she served until 1979 when sold to Indonesia as *Ek Daya Samudera.* She was broken up at Kaohsiung in 1984. This aerial photograph clearly shows how the bulwarks were set in from the side. *[Fotoflite incorporating Skyfotos]*

Views of two liquefied gas tankers owned by Nile Steamship Co. Ltd. Above is the ill-starred but long-lived *Teviot,* built at Burntisland for bareboat charter to local company George Gibson and Co. Ltd. She was sold in 1979, and became *Rudi M,* but her new owners had little use from her, as whilst lying in the Thames in November 1979 her insulation became saturated, a seemingly trivial accident which left her a constructive total loss. She was repaired, although suffering fire damage during the work. With her gas tanks removed, she became the effluent tanker *Kingsabbey,* but her misadventures were not over, and she became notorious for slicing through Southend Pier in June 1986. These calamities do not seem to have affected her longevity, and the 1966-built tanker is still carrying effluents as *St. Stephen,* a name given her in 1988. *[Fotoflite incorporating Skyfotos]*

The *Clerk-Maxwell* was a product of Hawthorn Leslie and was chartered to Houlder Brothers and Co., and is seen in the funnel colours of Ocean Gas Transport. Her career was relatively straightforward, and although owned at times by other Furness subsidiaries - including Shaw, Savill - she retained her name until scrapped at Aviles, Spain in 1986. *[Fotoflite incorporating Skyfotos]*

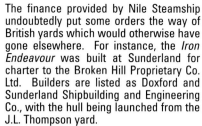

The finance provided by Nile Steamship undoubtedly put some orders the way of British yards which would otherwise have gone elsewhere. For instance, the *Iron Endeavour* was built at Sunderland for charter to the Broken Hill Proprietary Co. Ltd. Builders are listed as Doxford and Sunderland Shipbuilding and Engineering Co., with the hull being launched from the J.L. Thompson yard.

Subsequent names were *Andromachi* (1983), *Kapitan Ziya Somnez* (1990) and *Ocean Blue* (1992). She became one of a distesssing number of bulk carriers to have foundered due to stress of weather. On 26th May 1993 *Ocean Blue* sank after taking on water 70 miles south of Port Elizabeth whilst on a voyage with coal from Richard's Bay to Antwerp. Only 16 of the 33 crew were rescued.

[J.Y. Freeman, courtesy G.R. Scott]

The *Manchester Concorde* from Smith's Dock Co. Ltd., Middlesbrough was one of a group of pioneering containerships designed by Manchester Liners Ltd. for their Canadian services. They were built to the maximum size allowed by the Manchester Ship Canal, whose entrance *Manchester Concorde* is cautiously approaching. Sold to Taiwan buyers in 1982 and renamed *Char Lian,* she was soon scrapped, the breakers at Kaohsiung completing their work by the end of 1983. [J. and M. Clarkson]

The geared bulker *Bernes* was completed by Lithgows (1969) Ltd., the yard which had long since founded Nile Steamship Co. Ltd. Charterers were Tenax Steamship Co. Ltd., the British offshoot of the mighty Norwegian-based Jebsen group, whose distinctive funnel colours she wears. *Bernes* was sold in 1980, and has subsequently carried the names *Marina di Alimuri* (until 1989), *Boem* and since 1993 *Guang Shun*. [A. Duncan, courtesy G.R. Scott]

Kurdistan is seen at Wellington on 16th December 1976. She was built by Swan, Hunter at Hebburn as *Frank D. Moores* to serve an oil refinery which was to be built by the Newfoundland Refining Company at the wonderfully-named Come by Chance. She and three other tankers were chartered to Common Brothers, and traded wherever they could whilst completion of the refinery was awaited. Sadly, Newfoundland Refining went bankrupt, leaving Common Brothers to find work for the tankers in a depressed market. They were given traditional Common Brothers' names, *Frank D. Moores* becoming *Kurdistan* in 1976 and then *Simonburn* in 1979 after a new bow had been fitted when the original had fallen off in a collision with ice in the Cabot Strait. Common Brothers eventually disposed of the four tankers, but were badly hit financially by the Newfoundland debacle, and never completely recovered. The *Kurdistan* became the Liberian *Aura Bravery* and as *Seabravery* is still afloat.

[J. and M. Clarkson]

1. NILE 1919-33

O.N. 141932 5,696g 3,618n 9,450d 423.5 x 56.0 x 28.7 feet.

T. 3-cyl. by J.G. Kincaid and Co. Ltd., Greenock; 279 NHP, 3,000 IHP, 11 knots.

1.10.1919: Launched by Lithgows Ltd., Port Glasgow (Yard No. 715).

11.1919: Completed.

21.11.1919: Registered in the ownership of the Nile Steamship Co. Ltd. (Glen and Co., managers), Glasgow as NILE.

20.11.1933: Sold to the Brynymor Steamship Co. Ltd. (Ambrose, Davies and Matthews Ltd., managers), Swansea.

1933: Sold to Jugoslavenska Plovidba D.D., Susak, Yugoslavia and renamed SOKOL.

1939: Sold to Compania Panamena de Vapores Ltda., Panama (Th. and N. Coumantaros Ltd., Piraeus, managers) and renamed RIO GRANDE.

31.7.1940: Registered in the ownership of the Ministry of Shipping, London (Larrinaga Steamship Co. Ltd., Liverpool, managers) as EMPIRE BLANDA.

3.2.1941: Sailed from Halifax for Grangemouth with a cargo of steel, scrap and explosives, in convoy HX107.

18.2.1941: Straggling with engine trouble.

19.2.1941: Torpedoed and sunk by the German submarine U 69. There were no survivors from the 39 crew and 1 distressed British seaman.

21.3.1941: Register closed.

2. JUTLAND 1951-1953

O.N. 165992 5,237g 3,059n 447.6 x 56.2 x 24.9 feet.

T. 3-cyl. by Rankin and Blackmore Ltd, Greenock; 2,100 IHP, 11 knots.

26.8.1940: Launched by Lithgows Ltd., Port Glasgow (Yard No. 938) for Dornoch Shipping Co. Ltd., Glasgow (Lambert Brothers Ltd., London, managers) as COULBEG.

11.1940: Completed.

1951: Owners became the Nile Steamship Co. Ltd. (Glen and Co. Ltd., managers), Glasgow and renamed JUTLAND.

1953: Sold to the Trafalgar Steamship Co. Ltd. (Tsavliris (Shipping) Ltd., managers), London and renamed MARIANTHE.

1955: Sold to the Berna Steamship Co. Ltd. (S. Catsell and Co. Ltd., managers), London, renamed BERNA.

1958: Repossessed by Tsavliris (Hellas) Maritime Co. Ltd., Piraeus (Tsavliris (Shipping) Ltd., London, managers) and renamed MARIANTHE TSAVLIRIS.

1965: Owners became Kantara Shipping Ltd., Limassol (Tsavliris (Shipping) Ltd., London, managers) and renamed FREE MERCHANT.

9.6.1967: Sprang leak in a storm 700 miles from Colombo in position 9.11 north by 68.13 east whilst on a voyage from Beirut for Yokohama with a cargo of scrap. Abandoned, she settled by the stern, broke in two and sank the next day in position 9.11 north by 68.11.5 east.

Left: Photos of *Nile* under British ownership have proved elusive: this is her owned by Jugoslovenska Plovidba D.D. as *Sokol*. [Ivor Rooke collection]

Below: Nile's *Jutland* is seen here under her original name of *Coulbeg* in the colours of Lambert Brothers, her managers. [A. Duncan, courtesy Ivor Rooke]

3. DORNOCH/DUNROBIN/VENNACHAR 1952-1959
O.N. 165959 5,186g 3,075n 9,200d 448.5 x 56.2 x 24.8 feet.
T. 3-cyl. by Rankin and Blackmore Ltd., Greenock; 2,350 IHP, 11 knots.
12.12.1938: Launched by Lithgows Ltd., Port Glasgow (Yard No. 915) for Dornoch Shipping Co. Ltd., Glasgow (Lambert Brothers Ltd., London, managers) as DORNOCH
2.1939: Completed.
1952: Owners became the Nile Steamship Co. Ltd. (Glen and Co. Ltd., managers), Glasgow.
1956: Managers became Harrisons (Clyde) Ltd., Glasgow and renamed DUNROBIN.
1957: Renamed VENNACHAR.
21.10.1959: Arrived at Osaka from Aruba.
14.11.1959: Breaking up began by Banno Tsusho K.K., Osaka at Kinoe Hiroshima.

4. NAESS TALISMAN/NORDIC TALISMAN 1967-1978
O.N. 309852 40,919g 26,554n 72,072d 242.68 x 31.75 x 18.29 metres.
Sulzer 9RD90 type 9-cyl. 2SCSA oil engine by Fairfield-Rowan Ltd., Glasgow; 20,700 BHP, 15 knots.
4.8.1966: Launched by Lithgows Ltd., Port Glasgow (Yard No. 1157) for the Nile Steamship Co. Ltd., Glasgow as NAESS TALISMAN.
2.1967: Completed and demise chartered to Associated Bulk Carriers Ltd., London.
1974: Renamed NORDIC TALISMAN.
1978: Sold to Eddie Steamship Co. Ltd. (W.H. Eddie Hsu, managers), Taipei, Taiwan and renamed PANAMAX JUPITER.
1980: Owners became the United Overseas Marine Corporation, Monrovia (W.H. Eddie Hsu, Taipei, managers) and renamed BALTIC NEPTUNE.
1983: Owners became the Outeroceans Navigation Corporation Ltd. (W.H. Eddie Hsu, managers), Taipei and renamed PANAMAX CENTAURUS.
1.5.1984: Laid up at Kaohsiung.
29.12.1984: Bridge severely damaged by fire. Sold to Nan Sin Steel Enterprise Co. Ltd.
31.5.1985: Breaking up began in Taiwan.

Two views of Nile's third ship, as *Dornoch* (above) and as *Vennachar* (right) at Vancouver on 20th May 1959, only a few months before she went for scrap. Nile Steamship did not have their own funnel colours, and ships were painted in the livery of their managers, in this case Harrisons (Clyde) Ltd. Note how her superstructure has been modified between the two views. *[Above: A. Duncan, courtesy G.R. Scott; right F.W. Hawks, courtesy G.R. Scott]*

THE DEVELOPMENT OF OFFSHORE SUPPORT VESSELS Part 1
Peter Wynne

It is difficult to imagine that any port in the world has not been visited at some time by a vessel that is involved in offshore oil and gas exploration and exploitation since operations began in the 1950s and 1960s. The offshore support vessel is probably the best known and most easily identifiable of all the vessels that are involved in the offshore oil industry. With the bridge and accommodation well forward on a forecastle and a flat, open deck equipped for the carriage of deck cargo, the design is quite distinctive. Bright colours are also an aid to identification.

These vessels can be classified according to their design and capability; but they are all used for one main purpose - supply. Derivatives are, for example, supply, tug/supply, platform supply and anchor-handling tug/supply.

It should be remembered that, apart from a few exceptions, offshore support vessels are chartered for as short a period as one return trip to a rig or platform, or may be on long-term charters. When a definite task cannot be assigned a time period, the vessels are chartered by the day. Funnel colours are almost never repainted for long-term charters, although many vessels have been noted sporting plaques with the charterer's logo affixed to the sides of the superstructure.

Origins: southern USA
The concept of the supply vessel is a hybrid and has been improved and modified since the first vessels were built in the early 1950s. The earliest were developed in the southern United States and the design can be traced back to the chartered fishing vessels which provided the initial support for offshore oil operations.

Exploration for oil started in the swamps and marshes of South Louisiana in the 1930s where supplies were carried by small motorboats or, where the water was deeper, by fishing vessels. The latter were under 100 feet in length with bridge forward and a large open working deck and square open stern. This is still the staple design of fishing vessels in many parts of the United States and, although size and equipment has vastly improved, the modern versions of this vessel can be seen in many ports of the world.

Before the first oil production platform built out of sight of land was constructed during 1947 in shallow water offshore from the State of Louisiana, the need for 'large' supply vessels was not great. The first vessels built were less than 100 feet in length and had very little accommodation.

The first supply vessel has clearly been defined as the *Ebb Tide*, built in 1955. The concept - and I use the term lightly, rather than 'design' - has been attributed to the President of Ocean Drilling and Exploration Company: Alden J. LaBorde, affectionately known as 'Doc'. He understood the need for vessels that could carry supplies to his company's rigs out at sea and the concept was drawn up,

but he was not a seaman or even a designer. In fact, the hull was built to the design that is now the norm, but the bridge and engines are reported to have been recovered from an old tug. The *Ebb Tide* was 127 feet long and 27 feet wide.

Within a very short time *Ebb Tide* was proving its worth and further vessels followed, which formed the nucleus of Tidewater Marine Services fleet, established by Doc LaBorde and nine colleagues on the basis of the success of the design of the first offshore support vessel.

The supply vessel grows: the Gulf type
As trips became longer the need for cabin space grew and the accommodation block on the forecastle developed. Eventually, a length of 180 feet became the norm and was known in the industry as the Gulf type. Initially, the vessels were designed with squat rectangular funnels on the outer edges of the open cargo deck set three quarters aft. Below decks bulk cargo tanks - for powders such as cement and barites - were incorporated into the hull. Also, bulkheads formed cargo tanks for fluids such as fresh water, drilling water and fuel oils. Some were even fitted with additional tanks on the after deck. Navigational equipment was very basic - there was no real need for it! In the early days navigators used the existing rigs as markers. The seamanship of the crews was beyond question: after all, they had been working in the area for generations catching fish. The early designs were twin-screw vessels with low horsepower - in many cases under a total of 1,000 BHP - with a low freeboard. Experience in the deeper waters of the Gulf of Mexico soon lead to some changes in the basic design.

The developments in design and incorporation of modern equipment are quite evident when one compares the *Palex Service* of 1962 and *Endeavor* of 1964 and *Sea Serve 201* of 1965 with *Milano Service* of 1968. These four are examples of the Gulf type and the basic hull design can still be seen in the *Calico Jack* of 1974 with funnels mounted on the forecastle.

The exploration for and exploitation of offshore oil and gas in the European theatre was almost totally in the hands of US companies in the early stages. But, as the operations gained momentum, some European companies started to diversify and create new divisions or subsidiary companies whereby they could build and operate support vessels with a view to employing their own nationals rather than Americans. In the mid-1960s such companies were formed in Denmark, France, Germany, the Netherlands, Norway and the United Kingdom. The vessels were ordered mainly from shipyards that specialised in coasting vessels, barges, tugs and fishing vessels. In many cases the lines of the supply vessels could be related to fishing vessels with considerable sheer at the bow. Others were almost devoid of sheer and thus appeared to be low in the water. What was noticeable was that all of the vessels were Gulf types.

Deeper water, bigger vessels

In the early days of oil exploration the operations were concentrated in the southern area of the North Sea. However, seismic exploration reports showed that there were considerable deposits in deep water between the east coast of Scotland and Norway. As the exploration phase started in this area it quickly became evident that the Gulf type supply vessel was not appropriate for these operations as their hull design was not suitable for the heavy seas and rough weather that could be encountered. There have been reports of vessels encountering rough seas and water entering the exhausts in the squat funnels and thus stopping one of the engines. This was too great a risk to take when the vessel was in close proximity to an exploration rig, especially if the vessel should collide with the rig. The loss of both rig and supply vessel could result and the aftermath could be catastrophic.

The result was the development of designs in co-operation with shipyards to produce vessels with higher freeboard and larger forecastles and superstructure blocks. This produced a more sea-friendly vessel, which was also less prone to water washing over the open after deck. The most important feature of the improved design was that the funnels were now moved forwards to the forecastle and in some instances partially incorporated into the superstructure itself. Both US and European supply vessel operating companies constructed vessels to this development of the earlier designs.

Tug/supply vessels

As exploration moved into deeper waters the design of drilling rig changed and the semi-submersible type became the norm. These rigs were mainly unpowered and therefore required towing from location to location. The demand for vessels to assist in this operation soon outstripped the availability of deep-sea tugs. The supply vessels' owners realised that there was an opportunity to enhance the capability of the supply vessel and use it as a tug. The tug/supply vessel and the anchor-handling tug/supply vessel were thus developed. Towing winches were installed during construction and the positioning of the funnels close to the superstructure was imperative to avoid the tow wires becoming fouled.

To be continued.

Right: An early Gulf type, the *Palex Service* of 1962. Note the towing winch mounted aft of the bridge deck.

Below: *Endeavor* of 1965.

Sea Serve 201 of 1965, photographed at Valetta in January 1987.

Milano Service of 1968.

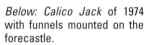

Below: Calico Jack of 1974 with funnels mounted on the forecastle.

Top: *Resolute* of 1973. The hull form is the same as the Gulf type but with funnels.

Middle: seen sailing from Aberdeen, *Arctic Seahorse* of 1973 is a Gulf type with funnels on the main deck. The towing winch is clearly visible.

Bottom: *Uco XI* of 1972: a Gulf type with exhausts set aft on the main deck.

Above: *Lowland Blazer* of 1966, launched as the *Lady Brigid*. In her case builders J. Bolson of Poole have incorporated some aspects of coaster design.

Below: *Nova Shore* of 1969. Again, the engine room uptakes are very small and are painted black.

Above: *Aberdeen Blazer* was launched in 1965 as the *Lady Alison*. Her builders, Hall, Russell of Aberdeen, have clearly incorporated some aspects of fishing vessel design.

Below: *Tropic Shore* of 1969. The engine room uptakes are very small and are painted grey. The 'funnel' markings are actually painted on the bulwarks.

Above: *Volans* of 1965 was launched as *Lady Anita*. Note the modified funnels.

Below: *Lady Lorna* of 1970. The trend to move the funnels towards the superstructure has started, although they are still very small

Above: *Suffolk Shore* of 1967 sailing from Great Yarmouth. She is clearly a British version of the US Gulf type with large, squat funnels.

Below: *Decca Mariner*, launched in 1965 as *Lady Laura*, again with funnels modified.

Above: Arriving at Fleetwood in August 1977, *Stirling Rock* of 1974 is a true British development of a Gulf type supply vessel.

Below: *Oil Producer* of 1972. A British Gulf type which was modified by raising the bulwarks on the forecastle to keep her dry. Note the A frame aft.

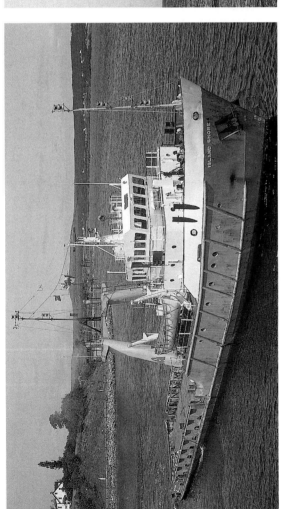

Above: the twin-funneled *Island Shore* of 1969.

Below: *Seaforth Hero* of 1973 sailing from Great Yarmouth. She is another British version of the Gulf type capable of towing/anchor handling.

Above: a German-built Gulf type, *Spitalertor* of 1971. Note the mast and derrick.

Below: *Norindo Sun* of 1975. One of 18 Norwegian Gulf types built in various shipyards in Holland.

Above: *Doventor* of 1973. Another German-built Gulf type with twin funnels.

Below: *Eko Truck* of 1975. A Norwegian-owned Gulf type, built to a standard shipyard design in Germany.

BRITISH LINERS - GREEK TRAMPS Part 2
Malcolm Cooper

Elder, Dempster

Elder, Dempster was the largest of the Royal Mail Group companies in terms of ships owned and had been the biggest participant in the post-war investment spree. The company purchased no fewer than 24 War standards (thirteen War As and Bs, eight War Ns, two War Cs, and one War F), as well as two Japanese-built War-type vessels. Elder, Dempster had continued to add tonnage throughout the 1920s, and when the depression struck was in the process of introducing the eight-strong 'Explorer' class of motorships. The company's West African business was in more robust shape than the troubled South American lines, and would be rescued relatively easily by Holts during the Group restructuring. It was, however, heavily over-invested. With foreign lines taking a larger part of the cargo, and British trade reduced by the decision of Lever Brothers to enter shipping through the United Africa company (later Palm Line), Elder, Dempster simply had far too many ships. It thus proved to be the single biggest supplier of tonnage to Greek tramp owners.

Two pre-war ships went to the Greek flag at the beginning of the depression. The 1907-built *Benin* was sold to Pateras of Chios in 1929, and traded for three years as *Haralampos P.* under Rethymnis and Kulukundis management before going to Spanish breakers. *Palma*, built in the same year, was sold to T. Fonaris, another R and K client, in January 1930 but only lasted as *Fonaris* for another year and a half before being broken up in Italy.

In 1933-34, however, there was a mass sale of War standard tonnage. Greek buyers took no fewer than seven of the Elder, Dempster B-class (a mixture of War As and Bs), two of the War Ns, as well as both of the ex-Japanese J class and their sole War F1. Rethymnis and Kulukundis, usually acting through the Tramp Ship Development Company, was the moving force behind most of these sales. *Bathurst* went to B.E. Benierakis of Patras as *Kostis*. She would survive until 1951 when, after two further name changes, she foundered following a grounding in Norwegian waters. *Boutry* entered the R and K Greek fleet as *Mount Rhodope*, became one of only four Mount ships to survive the Second World War, and was eventually broken up as *Captain Giorgis* in 1960. *Bata*, *Badagry* and *Bompata* all went to R and K's new British-flagged fleet as *Tower Abbey*, *Tower Bridge* and *Tower Dale* respectively. All were sold on at a profit after the depression, the first to Australian interests, the second to the Ben Line and the third to Finland. Each eventually ended their days under other owners, one being sunk in 1944 as the Japanese *Utide Maru*, another broken up as the Hong Kong-registered *Sigma Trader* in 1958, and the last broken up as the Panamanian *Kefalos* a year later. *Barracoo* went to Nicolas Estathiou of Piraeus as *Michalakis*, but was also lost under Japanese colours in the Second World War, this time as *Kusuyama Maru* in 1943. The last of the sisters, *Burutu* went to another small Greek owner, D. Inglessi Fils of Samos as *Demetrios Inglesses* and would survive without further name change until broken up in 1959.

Photographed in the Mersey by Basil Feilden, *Kostis* was formerly Elder, Dempster's *Bathurst,* launched by Caird and Co. Ltd., Greenock in 1919 as *War Alyssum.* She became *Diamantis* in 1939, surviving the war only to suffer a serious fire and explosion off Canada in July 1948. Perhaps surprisingly, the 29-year old ship found a new owner and was put back into service as *Thorros.* Her end was not greatly delayed however; on 29th November 1951 *Thorros* went aground near Honningsvaag whilst carrying timber from Archangel to Cardiff. She was refloated in December, but sank soon after. *[Basil Feilden, courtesy G.R. Scott]*

Seen here in the ownership of Margaronis Brothers, *Mount Rhodope* was formerly Elder, Dempster's *Boutry,* launched in 1919 as the War B type *War Gull* by Irvine's Shipbuilding and Dry Dock Co. Ltd., West Hartlepool. In 1957, the 38-year old steamer could still find a buyer, and Potamianos Brothers got another three years' trading from her as *Captain Giorgis.* She was broken up at Piraeus in 1960. *[G.R. Scott collection]*

Bompata was built for Elder, Dempster by Harland and Wolff Ltd. at Belfast, driven by two steam turbines geared to a single screw. She is seen after her sale for just £8,500 in July 1934 when she became the British *Tower Dale.* A new triple expansion engine was fitted for £12,000, and she was then sold in October 1935 for £36,500 to Finnish owners who renamed her *Navigator.* Surviving the war, she went back to Greek owners in 1956 as *Kefalos,* and was sold and renamed *Falkos* for her last voyage to breakers at Osaka at the end of 1959. *[A. Duncan, courtesy G.R. Scott]*

Greek tramps in the River Plate grain trade were frequent visitors to Buenos Aires, where *Michalakis* was photographed arriving on 6th November 1935. A product of R. Thompson and Sons Ltd., Sunderland, she had been completed as *Barracoo* for Elder, Dempster late in 1919. Another bargain, she cost her Greek owners just £6,225 in August 1933. In 1939 they sold her, undoubtedly at a handsome profit, to Yamashita Kisen K.K. of Kobe. As *Kusuyama Maru* she was torpedoed and sunk by the US submarine *Tunny* off Formosa on 8th February 1943. *[J. and M. Clarkson]*

In another Buenos Aires view, *Demetrios Inglesses* departs under the care of tugs on 6th January 1934. She had been completed in 1918 for the Shipping Controller by the Sunderland Shipbuilding Co. Ltd. as *War Swan,* and acquired by Elder, Dempster as *Burutu* in 1920. Laid up in the River Dart in 1930, she was sold in February 1934 to become *Demetrios Inglesses* (a name which 'Lloyd's Register' renders *Dimitrios Inglessis*). She was broken up as this at Osaka 25 years later. *[J. and M. Clarkson]*

The two War Ns also went to small owners, *New Georgia* to Nausicaa Shipping as *Penelope* and *New Mexico* to S.G. Razis as *Andreas*. The first would have a long and varied career before being broken up as *Atlantic Carrier* in 1959, but the second would be sunk by an Italian submarine in 1942. The Tramp Ship Development Co. bought both the Japanese-built ships. *Jebba* entered the Greek flag as Xilas Brothers' *Thalia*, to be sunk by Otto Kretschmer's U 99 in the SC7 convoy debacle in October 1940. No permanent owner could be found for *Jekri*, and like several other of the poorly-regarded Japanese Wars, she met an early end at the shipbreakers, going to Genoa for demolition in September 1933. *Fantee*, Elder, Dempster's sole War F1, was another addition to the R and K Greek fleet, serving as *Akti* of Kassos Steam Navigation Co. until lost after a collision with Hamburg South America Line's *La Plata* off Ushant in December 1938.

Fantee, sold for £9,000, brought the largest of what was a very inadequate series of returns for her former shareholders. The Japanese pair each realized less than half of that sum. The B and N class vessels were generally sold for between £6,000 and £7,000. Another indication of the extent to which these sales benefited the Greek buyers at the expense of the British sellers can be gained from the case of *Badagry/Tower Bridge*, which was sold on to the Ben Line in 1935 for £18,500.

Above: showing the trade mark triangular counter stern of the War N type, *Penelope* departs from Buenos Aires on 11th December 1935. She was launched as *War Triumph* by Harland and Wolff Ltd. but was completed in August 1919 for Elder, Dempster as *New Georgia*. Lay up at Dartmouth in 1930 was followed by sale for just £6,750 in March 1933. The name *Penelope* gave way to *Penelopi* just before the Second World War, and sufficed until sale to Hong Kong owners in 1956 saw her become *Pacific Carrier*. Within months a change of heart saw her become *Atlantic Carrier*. She was demolished at Mukaishima, Japan in 1959, at the age of forty. *[J. and M. Clarkson]*

Below, *Thalia* displays another trade mark of a War standard type, the triangular cross trees favoured by Japanese yards who built to British and Japanese account during and after the First World War. As *War Lion* she was completed by Kawasaki at Kobe, and sold to Elder, Dempster in October 1919. She fetched just £4,000 when sold in March 1933 after three years laid up. Seen here at Montevideo on 12th October 1936, *Thalia* was torpedoed and sunk on 19th October 1940. *[J. and M. Clarkson]*

The Northumberland Shipbuilding Co. Ltd. at Howden designed and built the War F1 type, which continued in production after the war. Seen above at Cape Town is Elder, Dempster's only example, the *Fantee,* completed in 1920. She was sold in March 1933 after a short lay up, to become *Akti* seen right arriving at Avonmouth. The Greek flags painted fore and aft may be an indication of neutrality during the Spanish Civil War. *[Above: A. Duncan; right: G.R. Scott collection]*

Furness-Houlder

Furness-Houlder, although a large and diversified shipping group, had managed its post-war modernization programme far more conservatively than Royal Mail. While it had to trim its sails in the depression, its restructuring was far more measured and far less crisis-driven than that of its rival. The group closed down its two Houlder-managed tramp subsidiaries, British Empire and Empire Transport, selling off a total of 17 largely pre-war ships for scrap or further trading. These vessels are outside the scope of this article, but it is worth noting that eight ended up under the Greek flag. *Indian Transport, Queensland Transport, Victorian Transport, Orange River, Derwent River, Gambia River,* and *Sagama River* were sold directly to Greek interests, while *Egyptian Transport* was sold on to a Greek owner by her original purchaser Eric Moller.

Disposals from the liner fleets were more modest, although like the Royal Mail case some were of ships which under other circumstances might have served longer in company colours. Manchester Liners sold the 1913-built *Manchester Civilian* to S.G. Razis of Argostoli in May 1933.

She served Razis as *Tasis* for two years before being sold to the Vergottis-managed Myrtoon Steamship Co. in 1935. Seized by the Vichy French in 1940, she was renamed *Equateur,* a name changed to *Bari* when seized in turn by the Italians two years later. As *Bari* she was sunk at Naples by Allied air attack in 1943. The war also claimed the other single Greek purchase from a Furness Group company. Houlder's *Oaklands Grange,* built a year before *Manchester Civilian* to the same basic design, was sold to M.N. Piangos of Andros in 1934. Renamed *Nicolaos Piangos,* she was bombed off Harwich in October 1941.

The other three Greek acquisitions from Furness all came from the Prince Line. Two had actually started life as tramps. *Siberian Prince* had been built in 1915 as *Baron Lovat* for Hogarth, only changing name and occupation two years later. *Korean Prince* had been completed two years later as Common Brothers' *Hindustan,* being sold to Prince Line in early 1918. Only *Persian Prince,* delivered in July 1918, and thus marginally the most modern of the three, had actually been designed for Prince Line service. Each was sold to a different medium-sized Greek owner in 1933-34.

Siberian Prince went to Leonidas Embiricos as *Dunavis*, *Korean Prince* to the Pateras family of Chios as *Diamantis*, and *Persian Prince* to A.D. Stathatos as *Ann Stathatos*. Only the last named survived the Second World War. *Dunavis* went to the Italian flag in 1939 as *Arlesiana* and was found sunk at Tunis when the Allies occupied it in 1943 (her hulk subsequently being raised and towed to the Tyne for demolition). *Diamantis* was an early casualty of the U-boat offensive, being sunk by *U 35* off Land's End in October 1939. *Ann Stathatos* sailed on in Greek colours until 1951 and was finally broken up as the Italian *Cadore* in 1959.

Interestingly enough, Prince Line got slightly better prices for its ships than the Royal Mail companies. *Siberian Prince* and *Persian Prince*, each sold in November 1933, realized £11,250 and £11,500 respectively. While this was still likely to have meant a significant book loss on the partially-depreciated value of the ships, it was clearly to the company's advantage that it was not a forced seller. The ex-Prince ships were broadly similar in age and specification to the Elder Dempster Bs, two of which had been sold a few months earlier for £6,200-£6,225.

Above: *Oaklands Grange* had been built in 1912 by the Northumberland Shipbuilding Co. Ltd. She is seen below as *Nicolaos Piangos* arriving at Buenos Aires on 11th August 1937. *[Above: A. Duncan, R. Fenton collection; below: J. and M. Clarkson]*

P and O/British India Group

The PandO/British India Group had vied with Royal Mail in the expansion frenzy of the first quarter of the century, buying up a number of British companies and taking on a large number of over-priced War standards in 1919-1920. British India was actually the biggest single purchaser of War standard tonnage, having acquired five War As, sixteen War Bs, eight War Ds, six War Gs, and four Japanese War standards from the Shipping Controller. Not one of these ships found its way into Greek hands during the Depression, and there were in fact very few disposals by Group companies during this period. This was not because they were doing much better operationally than their rivals, but more because the Group had superior financial reserves off which to live (and with which to support profits) during the hard times.

The only two liners from Group companies to be sold to Greek tramp owners during the period actually came from the Union Steamship Co. of New Zealand. Like its parent businesses, Union tended to dispose of tonnage in the Far East, but when it was decided to sell the company's three redundant War Fs, only one actually went to a traditional buyer. The other two would eventually return to eastern waters, but passed through Greek hands first. *Waikawa* was bought by Rethymnis and Kulukundis and entered their British-flagged fleet as *Tower Ensign* in 1934. Like her ex-Elder, Dempster near-sisters, she was sold on again within a few years, ending her days when lost in the *Fort Stikine* explosion at Bombay as Wallem and Co.'s *Iran*. *Waihemo* went to N.G. Livanos as *Evinos,* also in 1934. She survived the war as the Panamanian *Rio,* before coming back to the Far East as the Japanese *Shokyo Maru,* the name under which she was scrapped in 1958.

Above: *Tower Ensign* seen on 13th December 1936 at Charlton on the River Thames. Her history is involved: laid down by the Northumberland Shipbuilding Co. Ltd. as *War Donjon,* she was completed as *Waikawa* in 1919. The name *Tower Ensign* was carried for just two years, and in 1937 she became *Huntress* for A.G. Hunter. Renamed *Ronin* under the Greek flag in 1939, she became *Iran* in 1941, only to be badly damaged in the *Fort Stikine* fire at Bombay on 14th April 1944. [*F.W. Hawks, courtesy G.R. Scott*]

Right: two Harrison ships are seen laid up in Preston Dock in May 1930, the *Orator* and *Electrician,* outboard of the Danish *Victoria* (4,500/1928) which is discharging timber from Vancouver.

Like *Electrician, Orator* was an acquisition from Rankin, Gilmour, formerly the *Saint Fillans*. She found a Far Eastern buyer and lasted until 1956. [*J. and M. Clarkson*]

T. and J. Harrison

Harrison's well-established Charente Steamship Co. Ltd. survived the depression years in good shape, the company having built up strong reserves and eschewed over-ambitious modernization after the First World War. It did, however, possess some surplus tonnage and was forced to make a series of disposals. Most of the larger ships sold were too big for general use and went to the scrapyard. Three smaller Harrison liners, however, found their way to Greek tramp owners during the slump years. *Electrician,* built in 1914 as *Saint Winifred* was a survivor of the Rankin and Gilmour fleet

taken over by Harrisons in 1918. She was sold in 1932 to L.M. Logothetis and M. Fakis of Andros for only £3,900. Renamed *Aghia Varvara* she survived for six years before being wrecked near Ushant. The other two were purchased by Maris A. Embiricos, one of the more active buyers of British liner tonnage outside of the Rethymnis and Kulukundis empire. The 1912-built *Intombi* (launched as *Actor*) was renamed *Maliakos,* and the 1914-built *Navigator* became *Lakonikos.* The latter was sunk by *U 89* in 1943, but the former soldiered on until 1956 when she was lost in collision as the Turkish *Sapanca*.

Top: *Electrician* sailing from Preston in 1932 after being sold and renamed *Aghia Varvara*. She had been built by Russell and Co. at Port Glasgow.

Below: Harrison's *Intombi* arriving at Preston to lay up in May 1930 (middle photograph) and in the Mersey as *Maliakos* after her sale in January 1931 (bottom), when she fetched just £4,250. Embiricos kept her until 1949 when she was sold to Turkey as *Saraykoy* and later *Sapanca*. She sank on 28th February 1956 after colliding with the Dutch *Blommersdijk* in the Scheldt. *[Middle: J. and M. Clarkson; bottom: Basil Feilden, courtesy G.R. Scott]*

Frederick Leyland

Frederick Leyland was one of a group of British companies taken over in the early years of the century by the J.P. Morgan-backed International Mercantile Marine Corporation (IMMC). Morgan's attempt to dominate the North Atlantic liner trade proved ill-considered, and the IMMC was a spent force well before the depression hit. The heavy slump in trade accelerated the sell-off of the group's assets. Although the name and goodwill of Leyland was eventually acquired by Blue Star, and Harrisons took over the vessels and goodwill of its Gulf of Mexico service, the remaining ships were sold off individually. Among the disposals were three cargo vessels destined to end their days in two of the larger Greek tramp fleets. Leonidas Embiricos took the 1914-built *Oranian*, renaming her *Tamesis*. She moved to a different branch of the Embiricos family in 1939, joining the larger fleet of Maris A. Embiricos and changing her name to *Pagatsitikos* (the second ex-British liner to carry the name). She lasted until March 1942, when she was sunk by the German raider *Thor* in the South Atlantic. The other two purchases were War standard Bs, both of which were bought by Livanos and Co. for their Theofano Maritime Co. Ltd. *Barbadian* was renamed *Axios* and *Bolivian* renamed *Alfios*. These two sisters were destined to suffer a common fate, the first being wrecked in 1944 and the second in 1946.

Top: *Tamesis* ex-Leyland's *Oranian*, a product of Napier and Miller Ltd., Glasgow. [G.R. Scott collection]

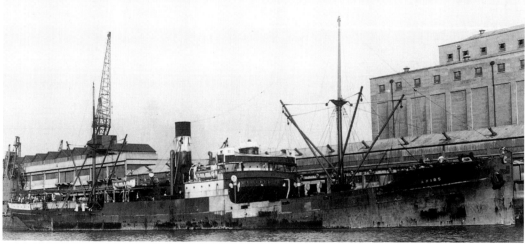

Middle: *Axios*, previously Leyland's *Barbadian*, had been laid down by Swan, Hunter as *War Tapir*. On 28th March 1944 she stranded at Sandheads whilst entering Calcutta with a cargo of cement from Port Okha. [A. Duncan, courtesy G.R. Scott]

Bottom: *Alfios, sister of Axios,* was previously *Bolivian,* having been intended to be *War Otter* when laid down by Irvine's Shipbuilding and Dry Dock Co. Ltd., West Hartlepool. Having survived the war, she was wrecked on 15th April 1946 on Sable Island whilst on a ballast voyage from Halifax to Glasgow. [G.R. Scott collection]

Nautilus Steam Shipping Co. Ltd.

The last of the major contributors to the Greek purchase of British liner tonnage was in some ways the saddest. Nautilus had been set up as a tramp concern in Sunderland in 1881 but had moved into the liner trade through purchase of the Gulf Line's conference rights in the west coast of South America trade. Still a small independent family firm at a time when much of the industry had moved into large groups, Nautilus was not strong enough to survive the heavy costs of post-war rebuilding and the subsequent prolonged slump in trade. The depression finished off the company and it was wound up with the loss of its entire share capital in 1931. The fleet was sold off gradually by the bank which had held a mortgage over it. The four oldest ships went to the shipbreakers, while a Chilean buyer took another two. The other four all went to Greek buyers. The most modern, the 1921-built *Pear Branch,* went to the Maris A. Embiricos

fleet as *Argolikos.* The other three all went to the same buyer, the London-based A. Lusi, who had just entered shipowning on his own account, operating his fleet under the Argostoli registry. The youngest was the 1910-built, clipper-stemmed *Cedar Branch,* which was renamed *Aenos.* The other two, *Hazel Branch,* completed in 1906 and *Cherry Branch,* built in 1909, were actually former Scottish tramps, having started life respectively as Bell Brothers' *Bellgrano* and Henderson and McIntosh's *Dunedin.* They were renamed *Vagliano* and *Zephyros.* *Vagliano* returned briefly to British colours when sold to Souters for Scrap and Build purposes in the mid-1930s. The other three ships were still sailing during the war, when *Aenos* became another Greek casualty of the SC7 convoy fiasco. *Zephyros* was wrecked off the Tyne in 1947 (and was pictured in *Record* 8, page 244), and *Argolikos* finally went to Japanese ship breakers in 1953.

Above: a fine view of *Argolikos,* ex-*Pear Branch,* in the Scheldt. The Palmers-built steamer survived the war to be broken up at Osaka in November 1953. *[Roy Fenton collection]*

Below: the clipper-bowed, Bartram-built *Cedar Branch* arriving at Avonmouth, and opposite page top as *Aenos,* following her sale to A. Lusi in 1932. *[Below: J. and M. Clarkson; opposite top: G.R. Scott collection]*

Middle: seen at Montevideo is Lusi's *Vagliano* ex-*Hazel Branch*, which had been built by Napier and Miller, Glasgow as *Bellgrano*. In 1936 *Vagliano* was bought for £8,000 by W.A. Souter and Co. Ltd. and broken up at Blyth under the 'Scrap and Build' scheme, which did not specify that owners had to trade in existing units of their own fleet. In return for breaking up *Vagliano* and two other acquisitions, Souters obtained loans to build the steamer *Hylton* (5,197/1936). *[J. and M. Clarkson]*

Bottom: The Connell-built *Zephyros,* ex-*Cherry Branch*, photographed on 16th July 1932 in the busy harbour at Buenos Aires. Behind her is Albyn Line's *Thistleglen* (4,750/1929). *[J. and M. Clarkson]*

The paddle steamer *Empress Queen* of 1907, the Steam Packet Company's fastest vessel until the arrival of *Ben-my-Chree* (3). The largest and fastest cross-channel paddle steamer ever built, she could carry 1,994 passengers and when new established a record for the Rock Light to Douglas Head passage of 2 hours 57 minutes. Whilst serving as a troop transport, on 1st February 1916 she stranded in fog off Bembridge, Isle of Wight and later broke up. *[Ballast Trust]*

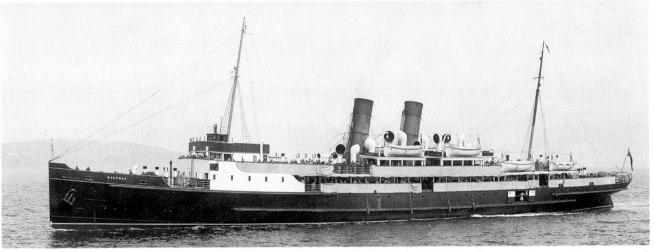

The completion of the turbine steamer *Manxman* in 1904 for the Midland Railway stimulated the Isle of Man Steam Packet Company to order their own turbine steamer. The Steam Packet Company bought the ship after her First World War service, and she served them faithfully - she is seen arriving at Douglas in June 1933 - until requisitioned early in the Second World War. War service included the Dunkirk evacuation, when she took 2,394 men off the beaches. She was laid up at Barrow-in-Furness after the war and broken up at Preston, where she arrived in tow on 9th August 1949. *[J. & M. Clarkson collection]*

Viking of 1905 was the Steam Packet's response to *Manxman,* and was herself a record breaker. Like her immediate predecessor, *Ben-my-Chree,* she also served as a seaplane carrier during the First World War, being renamed HMS *Vindex.* She survived this war, and the subsequent one, being returned to Steam Packet service after each conflict, and lasting until 1954. *[J. & M. Clarkson]*

BEN-MY-CHREE OF 1908
John Shepherd

The 1908 *Ben-my-Chree* on trials. *[Glasgow University Archives DC101/0944/Y1]*

Early steam turbines

It was in 1894 that Charles Parsons invented the steam turbine. Three years later he was able to demonstrate the turbine's effectiveness when his experimental torpedo boat, the *Turbinia,* charged through the lines of the 1897 British Naval Review at Spithead at an unprecedented speed of 34 knots.

The shipbuilder William Denny at Dumbarton on the Clyde saw the potential of the turbine and approached Charles Parsons. This led to the construction of the turbine steamer *King Edward* which was launched at Dumbarton on 16th May 1901. Denny put up most of the capital, providing some £24,200 and Parsons provided a further £8,000.

Such was the success of the *King Edward* that the South Eastern and Chatham Railway introduced a turbine steamer, *The Queen,* on the Dover Strait in 1903, and the first turbine steamer ever to visit the Isle of Man was the Midland Railway Company's *Londonderry* which called at Douglas on an excursion sailing from the newly opened port of Heysham on Saturday 13th August 1904. Two months prior to this visit, the Midland Railway Company had launched another new turbine steamer, the *Manxman,* at Vickers' Barrow yard on 15th June 1904. With a name like this she was obviously destined for the Heysham to Douglas route, in direct competition with the Isle of Man Steam Packet Company's long-established Fleetwood to Douglas service. The *Manxman* inaugurated the new service on 1st June 1905 and

advertised a scheduled crossing time of 2 hours 40 minutes. This was far superior to the Isle of Man Company's paddle steamers on the Fleetwood to Douglas run.

To counter this opposition the Isle of Man Steam Packet Company placed an order with Armstrong, Whitworth and Co. Ltd. of Newcastle-upon-Tyne for a new direct-drive turbine steamer which would be guaranteed to steam at least three-quarters of a knot faster than the *Manxman*. This was the Steam Packet Company's first turbine steamer, and the only vessel ever to be built for them on the north-east coast. She was named *Viking* at her launch on 7th March 1905 and ran her trials on 10th June when 23.53 knots was achieved. The *Viking's* maiden voyage was from Liverpool to Douglas on 26th June 1905 after which she became the mainstay of the Fleetwood to Douglas service

The new *Viking* quickly proved herself on the Fleetwood service and on 25th May 1907 crossed to Douglas, berth to berth, in 2 hours 22 minutes; a record which stood until the introduction of SeaCat services on 28th June 1994.

The 'crack' ship on the Isle of Man Steam Packet Company's Liverpool to Douglas service was the paddle steamer *Empress Queen.* She was launched from the Fairfield yard at Govan on 14th March 1897 and achieved 21.75 knots on her trials on 8th July. In the summer of 1898 the *Empress Queen* was averaging 3 hours and 5 minutes for the Liverpool to Douglas passage.

Ben-my-Chree probably in the Sloyne. *[J. & M. Clarkson]*

Ben-my-Chree of 1908

The success of the *Viking* led the Steam Packet Company to order in 1907 a larger turbine steamer from the Barrow yard of Vickers, Sons and Maxim Ltd. She was launched on 23rd March 1908 and named *Ben-my-Chree* (3). The new ship cost £112,000. Direct drive turbines built by Vickers at Barrow coupled to triple screws gave a trials speed of 24.26 knots, with 26.64 knots being achieved on one run of the measured mile at Skelmorlie on 8th August 1908. Going astern she could make 16.6 knots. The new *Ben* had a passenger certificate for 2,549 and carried a crew of 119. She could burn up to 95 tons of coal in a single day's steaming. The *Ben's* average time for her first season's sailings between the Bar Lightship and Douglas Head was an impressive 2 hours 24 minutes.

On 9th July 1909 the *Ben-my-Chree* made her fastest recorded passage on the Liverpool to Douglas service. She crossed from the Mersey Bar Lightship to Douglas Head in 2 hours 16 minutes and the complete passage, berth to berth, was made in 2 hours 57 minutes. The new *Ben,* according to the Steam Packet's centenary book, quickly earned the distinction of being *'the fastest and most luxuriously appointed channel steamer afloat'.*

On 11th June 1911 the *Ben-my-Chree* was challenged to a 'Round the Island' race with an early aircraft as part of the Douglas Jubilee Celebrations. The tiny aircraft, piloted by Graham White, had to land frequently to make adjustments and the *Ben* emerged the victor!

Early in the *Ben-my-Chree's* career, alleged racing in the Mersey channels caused a question to be put in Parliament by Mr Gershom Stewart MP to the President of the Board of Trade. In reply, Mr Winston Churchill said that he would write to the shipowners concerned. The evening arrivals of the *Ben* from Douglas and the Liverpool and North Wales Steamship Company's *La Marguerite* from Llandudno off the Rock Light had obviously been taken too

seriously! Both vessels were scheduled to arrive at Princes Stage at Liverpool within five minutes of each other, and friendly racing between the two companies' steamers did in fact take place right up to September 1962 when the *St. Tudno* made her last sailing.

The *Ben-my-Chree's* career on her designed route was short; from late August 1908 until early August 1914. The *Ben* was laid up for almost nine months each winter. Her large passenger capacity was not required except at the peak of the summer season, and she was an expensive ship to run. She lived a charmed existence during those six halcyon summers. There are no records of any groundings, collisions or other mishaps.

The outbreak of the First World War

The First World War began on 4th August 1914 in what should have been the peak of the summer seasonal traffic. Passenger arrivals at Douglas fell away drastically over the first weekend of August and at a special meeting of the Steam Packet Directors on 10th August it was decided to lay up the *Ben-my-Chree, Viking* and *Empress Queen* immediately.

The *Ben-my-Chree* entered Cammell Laird's wet basin at Birkenhead on 2nd January 1915 where her conversion to a seaplane carrier took place. A hangar was built, aft of her second funnel, to house six seaplanes which would be lifted in and out of the water by a crane. There was a flying-off platform forward, of about 60 feet in length. The *Ben* was soon to contribute to the development of naval aviation.

The *Ben-my-Chree* was commissioned on 3rd March 1915 and her first base was Harwich where she arrived on 28th April. The *Ben* was armed with four 12-pounders and four anti-aircraft guns. She carried four Short 184 seaplanes. Her complement was some 250, including flying crew and mechanics.

An early aircraft carrier

Taking off from the *Ben's* flying-off platform was indeed a precarious business. The *Ben* would head into the wind and work up to full speed. A plane would rev-up whilst a hook held it steady until it was released down the sloping 60-feet long runway over the bows. If the pilot could not gain sufficient lift his plane would fall into the sea and was likely to be rammed by the ship just seconds later! Following the *Ben-my-Chree's* conversion, she had considerably greater top hamper, and this vast windage made her difficult to handle. The runway proved inadequate for the planes, so in practice the *Ben* had to stop and lower the seaplanes into the water for take-off. This was a serious problem in action.

During the *Ben's* first months of war service, she also carried Sopwith Schneider floatplane fighters to intercept Zeppelins over the North Sea. These were single-seater biplanes, made of wood and fabric covered, and were lighter than the Short 184s and successful take-offs were eventually made from the *Ben's* flying-off platform.

By August 1915 the *Ben-my-Chree* was on her way to the Mediterranean. She was soon in action spotting for naval gunners in bombardments of Turkish positions during the Gallipoli campaign. She remained until the evacuation of Gallipoli when she was said to be the last British ship to leave.

Making aviation history in the Mediterranean

The *Ben-my-Chree's* place in aviation history was secured on 12th August 1915. One of the *Ben's* Short 184s spotted a 5,000 ton Turkish supply ship and attacked it from the air. The aircraft was piloted by Flight Commander C.H. Edmonds and he aimed a 14-inch Whitehead torpedo at his target at a range of 890 feet, having glided down to 15 feet above the water. The vessel was hit amidships and sunk. This was the first ever successful attack against a ship with a torpedo dropped from the air. In the five days following this success, two more torpedo attacks were launched by the *Ben's* aircraft against Turkish supply ships.

On 2nd September 1915 the *Ben-my-Chree* received an S.O.S. message from the troopship *Southland* of the Red Star Line and she rescued 815 people from the torpedoed liner in the Aegean Sea.

There was a once popular story that the *Ben-my-Chree* was loaded with ammunition and despatched round the Cape of Good Hope to service warships that were under orders to sink the German light cruiser *Königsberg* which was sheltering in the Rufiji Delta in Tanganyika (now Tanzania). She is reputed to have made this long voyage, from England to East Africa, at an average speed in excess of 22 knots, including stops for coaling. However, as surviving log fragments have shown, it would have been impossible for her

Two views of *HMS Ben-my-Chree*, seaplane carrier. In the lower photograph, at Mudros in November 1915, her mainmast is mounted on her hangar, with a kingpost aft to lift her seaplanes. *[Imperial War Museum SP995 and SP494]*

to have made the trip in the time between her North Sea operations and her main Mediterranean war work.

Towards the end of 1916 the *Ben* passed through the Suez Canal into the Red Sea where she bombarded enemy camps and bombed railways, before returning to the Eastern Mediterranean.

The loss of the 'Ben' - January 1917

On 11th January 1917 the *Ben-my-Chree* was anchored in a supposedly safe bay off the island of Castellorizo (off the south-west Mediterranean coast of Turkey). Unknown to the *Ben*, a Turkish battery had taken up position on the coast of mainland Turkey, about two miles away. The battery opened up on the *Ben-my-Chree* holing the petrol store which set the ship on fire. As the *Ben's* steering gear had also been put out of action by the shelling, it was impossible to move out of range. The *Ben-my-Chree* was abandoned after half an hour of shelling and one of her three motor-boats which was still intact was used to ferry her complement of 250 ashore. The *Ben* herself provided a 'shield' during this operation

The *Ben-my-Chree* continued to be shelled for about five hours until she settled in shallow water as a burned out hulk. The Master and the Chief Engineer later returned to the wreck and saved the ship's cat and two dogs.

The wreck of the *Ben-my-Chree* lay off Castellorizo until it was raised by the salvage steamer *Vallette* in 1920. It was then towed to Piraeus where, following examination, repairs were not considered possible. The story ended three years later when the hulk was towed to Venice in 1923 and demolished.

During her six short summer seasons as 'crack' ship on the Liverpool and Douglas service, the *Ben-my-Chree* had built up a tremendous reputation for herself. The Manx people had a genuine pride in the ship and there was real grief on the Island at the news of her loss.

Her two near sisters, the *Manxman* and the *Viking*, survived the First World War. Both, like the *Ben*, had been converted to seaplane carriers. After the War, the Isle of Man Steam Packet Company purchased the *Manxman* which survived until the completion of her Second World War service in 1949 when she was broken up by T.W. Ward at Preston. The *Viking* also survived the Second World War and returned to the Fleetwood and Douglas service in 1946. She remained a coal burner until the end and made her last voyage on 14th August 1954. Two days later she sailed for Barrow and the scrapyard of T.W. Ward.

Early turbine steamers - the first fast-craft

There is much talk these days about 'fast-craft'. This refers to the frail, fragile, claustrophobic, aluminium capsules which are the fashion of the day. In anything short of a flat calm they provide an appallingly uncomfortable ride for passengers, and with average berth-to-berth timings on the Liverpool to Douglas route rarely bettering 2 hours 50 minutes, today's 'fast-craft' are only about five minutes faster than the first turbine steamers of 90 years ago.

The real fast craft were the *Ben-my-Chree* of 1908, the *Viking* of 1905 and the *Manxman* of 1904. These splendid early turbine steamers provided a comfortable, reliable and fast crossing in all weathers, without any of the operating restrictions in wave heights of over three metres which make travelling by today's 'fast craft' nothing short of a lottery.

The *Ben-my-Chree* on fire off Castellorizo on 11th January 1917. *[Imperial War Museum SP201]*

Four views of the salvage of *Ben-my-Chree* in 1920. In the top photograph a cofferdam is completed. Far left is a view from the masthead, and near left shows the pumps working whilst divers seal the cofferdam. In the bottom view, *Ben-my-Chree* is being brought upright.
[National Maritime Museum]

239

Two views of the forlorn hulk of *Ben-my-Chree* on 11th November 1920. Like so many other ships before and since which have lain at Piraeus, she was awaiting a decision on her fate. Deemed not worth repairing, she was towed to Venice for demolition in 1923. *[J. & M. Clarkson]*

from Lloyd's Register, 1910:
BEN-MY-CHREE
Official number: 118605
Gross tonnage: 2,651   Nett tonnage: 1,733
Built by Vickers, Sons and Maxim Ltd. at Barrow-in-Furness in 1908
Length: 375ft   Breadth: 46.2ft
Engines: three steam turbines by Vickers, Sons and Maxim Ltd.

WHAT SHIP?

The accompanying illustration is from a postcard on sale for just £1 as the name of the vessel is not known and the card is creased, although this does not affect the image of the ship. There is nothing on the back to indicate when or where the photograph was taken and it has not been through the post.

It appears to show a yacht that has been taken into naval service. One can pick out at least 34 ratings and officers and a gun has been mounted on the after end. Astern of her are several smaller craft, one of which is numbered *ML344*.

Can any one identify this vessel?

EVERY PICTURE TELLS A STORY
John Naylon

Sic transit gloria - the former colonial clipper barque *Berean* lies beached in Falmouth harbour in 1910, at the end of her career, with only her fore and main lower masts and bowsprit standing.

Described by Basil Lubbock as 'The best known, as well as the fastest, of all Walker's barques ... the beautiful little *Berean*' was launched in August 1869 by W. Pile of Sunderland for Thomas Boss Walker of London (and originally of Scarborough). This was the year which saw the launch of such well-known tea clippers as the *Cutty Sark, Caliph, Norman Court* and *Wylo*. Pile contributed to this famous cohort with the *Lammermuir, Maitland, Undine* and *Deerhound* but he also built speedy vessels, including six for Walker, for the lesser Australian trades, which called for smaller tonnage than the main lines to Melbourne, Adelaide and Sydney.

T.B. Walker's connection with the Tasmanian and Queensland trades extended from 1851 to his death in 1894; over this period he operated thirty-one small brigs, snows, barques and full-riggers, all substantially less than 1,000 tons. A.H. Thurgar, who served in the *Berean*, writing in *Sea Breezes* (Old Series), Volume 4, 1922, said that all Walker's ships were smart sailers, carrying general cargo out from London and mostly wool home.

The *Berean* was built on similar lines to the tea clippers *Maitland* and *Undine,* of composite construction (an iron frame planked, like the *Cutty Sark*) and measured 526 nt and 542 gt on dimensions 160.5 x 30.2 x 17.2 feet. She was built at a time when composite construction was at the height of its popularity and the condition of her hull was testimony to the quality and durability of this type of building. To the end of her 41-year active career she never needed to be recaulked or her seams to be touched.

Altogether she was built to a very high specification. Her 43-foot raised quarterdeck was laid with New Zealand kauri pine planking extending the full length without a butt or a knot. All the deck fittings, houses, fife rails, skylights, bulwarks, boats and even the bunk boards and lining of the forecastle were of selected teak. For many years she carried fore and main skysails; but although stunsail irons were fitted the sails themselves were never carried since Walker had ascertained from his captains that the little extra speed they provided was not worth the trouble of handling them.

The *Berean* was commanded throughout her 28 years under the Red Ensign by Captain John Wyrill, himself a personality. First going to sea in 1850, he never served in a steamship. He circumnavigated the globe 36 times and he commanded sailing ships for 44 years - 42 of them in the Tasmanian trade, where both he and the *Berean* were immensely popular.

It was Captain Wyrill's boast that in his time in the *Berean* he had never been 90 days on passage, out or home. He generally left the West India Docks for Launceston in May and was back in the Thames about the following March. The *Berean* was too small to take full advantage of the strong westerlies of the Southern Ocean, but in moderate weather she showed she could more than hold her own with such notable flyers as the American clipper *Yosemite,* the Aberdeen White Star *Samuel Plimsoll,* the speedy four-master *Loch Carron,* the famous *Thermopylae,* and Green's *Melbourne* and *Windsor Castle* - all vessels twice her size and much more powerful. Her best outward passage to Launceston was 71 days pilot to pilot, 68 days land to land, and in 1881-2 she ran from Launceston to the Lizard in 79 days. She once went from the Equator to the Channel in 17 days and her first four passages out to Tasmania averaged 77 days.

According to Lubbock, the *Berean* was so free from accidents that Lloyd's underwriters offered to insure her at a specially reduced premium. Apart from a collision in the Thames when she was towing up from Gravesend, which damaged her bowsprit, figurehead and cutwater, her narrowest escape was in 1888 when she just missed going ashore on the Isle of Wight owing to Trinity House advising that the fixed oil light on St. Catherine's was to be replaced by an electric flash - and then not altering it.

It was a Thames collision, however, which finally ended the *Berean's* active career. After T.B. Walker died in 1894 his three remaining ships were sold, the *Berean* going in 1897 to H. Skougaard of Langesund, Norway (Captain Wyrill went to Hine's barque *Eden Holme* and continued in the Tasmanian trade). Skougaard owned eight small sailing vessels and two steamers, and like her stable mates the *Berean* was engaged for the next fourteen years in the rough and heavy ice trade from Norway to the Thames, usually berthing in the Regent's Canal Dock. On 8th April 1910 she was in collision with the steamer *Julia* of Danzig and was beached in a sinking condition near Gravesend. Condemned, she was patched up and towed to Falmouth. Our picture shows her with the windmill pump, obligatory in all Norwegian sailing vessels, at the foot of the main mast; but her composite hull was still sound enough for further service as a hulk.

PUTTING THE RECORD STRAIGHT

Letters, additions, amendments and photographs relating to articles in any issues of *Record* are welcomed. Letters may be lightly edited. E-mails are welcome, but senders are asked to include their postal address.

Passenger ships from the Wear

I found John Lingwood's piece on Sunderland (*Record* 19) very interesting. He rightly points out that the two motorships *India* and *Timor*, which Bartrams produced for the Companhia Nacional de Navegacao of Lisbon, were unusual among Wear-built ships in having substantial passenger capacity. In fact, this was not the original intention. In the period immediately after the Second World War, the Nacional company ordered several freighters from Bartrams. They were, however, being required by the Portuguese Government to provide two smallish passenger/cargo ships to maintain the subsidised colonial links with Goa, Macao and Timor. Accordingly, it was decided that the design of two of the freighters should be modified to satisfy this need. Over the years, the pair also made a number of voyages to the Portuguese possessions in West and East Africa, and latterly they were often used for trooping.

The Nacional company specified Doxford engines for a number of their ships. The hulls of the *India* and *Timor* were towed to the Tyne to have their engines installed by the North Eastern Marine Engineering Co. (1938) Ltd. and were then towed back to Sunderland.

The aerial photograph which you use of the *India* is revealing, but it is worth adding that pictures taken from a lower level emphasise that these ships had very streamlined superstructures and were, indeed, quite avant-garde for 1951. Bartrams are said to have made a loss on the contract to build them.
ANTHONY COOKE, Carmania Press, Unit 212, Station House, 49 Greenwich High Road, London, SE10 8JL

Caledonian corrections

Congratulations once again on yet another excellent issue.

In accordance with your stated desire to receive comments and corrections, may I draw your attention to the Cooper, of Kirkwall, ship *Express* (2) formerly John MacCallum's *Hebridean* (*Record* 19, page 174)? The dimension shown in the article are those of *Hebridean's* successor, *Hebrides* of 1898, and should have been 139.75 x 23.5 x 12.0 feet. The gross and net tonnages are correct for *Hebridean*.

With regard to the article on Bank Line engines, I was always under the impression that the Harland and Wolff Finnieston Engine Works was the local branch of the Belfast Engine Works with responsibility for servicing the ships built in the Govan Shipyard and, on occasion, ships built by A. and J. Inglis Ltd., a wholly-owned Harland subsidiary from 1919 until closure in 1962. It was a Mr Rebbeck, later Sir Frederick, who was manager at Finnieston in the 1920s prior to his promotion to Belfast as managing director of H. & W. Finally, it is somewhat misleading to say that Finnieston is near Glasgow as it is, in fact, a city centre district of that city.
IAN RAMSAY, Garmoyle, Main Road, Langbank, Renfrewshire PA14 6XP

Supremity or pursuasivity?

Since the article in *Record* 18 about this interesting ship, some facts have come to light that probably go some way to explaining one of the mysteries concerning her provenance. It could explain how the ship came to be built but still leaves unanswered the question of why permission was sought and granted in the first place.

While one could argue that the ship was not a standard for either owner or builder, a closer look at her dimensions and tonnage reveals that she bore a very strong resemblance to the Ministry standard *Icemaid* colliers. Most, if not all, of these were steamers and built at Grangemouth. Thus, in general terms, it could also be argued that externally she was indeed a standard type with alterations to the engine room arrangements and bunker spaces to take the diesel engine and the fuel oil. The crew accommodation was also altered and, to judge from a contemporary magazine article, it improved considerably on the standard. There appear to have been some delays during the building because ships with Goole yard numbers twenty beyond hers were completed at an earlier date.

This all begs the question of how a new type of diesel engine could be developed during the war when there were probably a number of other units of similar horsepower already being built elsewhere. Maybe it was argued that such development work was in the national interest. A more cynical view is that Everards were looking for a more powerful unit from their own stable and the average ministry inspector would be unable to tell the difference between an 'O' and a 'P' type under construction at the Newbury Diesel works.

One final point concerns the funnel colours. Pre-war and early post-war Everard ships had black funnels with the red and white flag motif. The yellow funnel did not appear until about 1950. But it is still an interesting fact that this departure from unrelieved grey was permitted at all. It all points to the work of some powerful persuasion.
KEN GARRETT, 3 The Grange, East Malling, Kent ME19 6AH

Doxford and/or Sunderland

Adam Scott Grey's letter in *Record* 19 provides a most interesting précis of Doxford's final years. The *Birchbank* and *Beaverbank* should indeed have been listed as having been built by Sunderland Shipbuilders Ltd. However, I cannot agree with his statement that all the Sunderland-built ships listed in part 2 of my article on Bank Line's post war vessels (*Record* 18) should have been so attributed. Both 'Lloyd's Register' and Harold Appleyard's WSS book on Bank Line give the builders of both *Fleetbank* and *Cloverbank*, the first pair of this group, as Doxford and Sunderland Ltd., who are also recorded as the engine manufacturers.
PAUL BOOT, 29 Meadowcroft, Heswall, Wirral, Cheshire CH60 1UT

Paul's letter gives the editors the opportunity to offer abject apologies to his co-author of the article 'Bank Engines', Roddie MacLeod, for whom we perpetrated the ultimate indignity which can be visited on a writer: having his name spelt wrong. In fact, we did it twice, spelling it two different ways. Sorry Roddie. Ed.

Bratton Castle located

With reference to the photograph of *Bratton Castle* (*Record* 19, page 141) 1 think I can throw a bit more light on the location.

I rather think that it was taken at the more southerly limit of the ship's usual run, i.e. entering the Victoria Basin, Cape Town Docks, the photo having been taken from the seaward side of the East Pier.

On the distant shore, just above the ship's forecastle head but abaft the two kingposts, is what appears to be Milnerton Power Station with two chimneys visible. Also, the ship is flying what would probably be a courtesy flag from the foremast head (which she would not do in UK waters). I cannot quite make out the letters on the notice board just above the car roof, but enlargement of the negative would probably show that the wording is in two languages, i.e. English and Afrikaans. Finally, the source of the photo (A. Duncan, who acquired a lot of the collection of the well-known Cape photographer, the late Robert Moffat Scott) also makes the Cape Town location more probable.

DAVID WITTRIDGE, 25 Fairlawn Close, Rownhams, Southampton S016 8DT

Rowhedge revisited

I was very interested in Mr Sargents letter (*Record* 18, page 86) regarding 'Every picture tells a story' on page 64 of *Record* 17. I lived in Rowhedge from age 1 until going away to sea in 1951 at 21.

In the First World War a pontoon bridge was built across the River Colne at exactly the spot where the coaster in the picture was beached. Can I suggest that the coaster may have been delivering the pontoons for the bridge? The bridge was built by the Royal Engineers, so this could account for the number of troops aboard the ship.

In my youth the shop visible in the photograph was a greengrocers. The building at the bow of the coaster is to this day almost unaltered as the pub called The Anchor. The house behind the funnel was that of the ferryman, whose ferry ran from where the coaster was beached to Wivenhoe. At the time the bridge spanned the river no shipping could proceed past the bridge to Colchester.

N.J. DAY, 7 Gosfield Road, Colchester, Essex CO2 0AS

Nits in 19

I do not like nit-picking, but as *Record* places such a high value upon accuracy I will mention a couple of points from issue 19.

Page 157. The *Blythe Star* was built by Duchesne & Bossière as ship number 101. This small shipyard eventually became part of an organisation called Sociètè Nouvelle des Ateliers et Chantiers du Havre.

Page 163. The *Watamurra* (as the *Asia Hero*) was delivered to shipbreakers at Jurong on 20.1.1977, with demolition commencing on either 22.1.1977 or 14.1.1977, according to which entry in *Marine News* one accepts (see *Marine News,* March and September 1977).

Regarding the fate of the *Wareatea, Record* states that '...although the *Bonahope's* Singapore registry was closed in 1984 she may well have gone much earlier'. I photographed *Bonahope* at Singapore in February 1977. I note that the ship was still in *Lloyd's*

Confidential Index in March 1985 and my records state 'broken up about 1991' although I cannot confirm this.

JOHN B. HILL, The Hollies, Wall, Hexham, Northumberland NE46 4EQ

Mechanical stoking and pulverised coal

Comments in Record *19, page 164 about how Manchester Liners pioneered the fitting of mechanical stokers in the 1930s prompted Alan McClelland to send us the following, part of his article in 'The British Shipbuilder' in February 1981.*

T. and J. Harrison of Liverpool, amongst the shrewdest of cargo ship operators, remained faithful to coal until the Second World War for what were sound economic reasons. The principal of these were their access to supplies of local Haydock, South Yorkshire and Brymbo coal on favourable contract terms, and the fact that their ships' furnaces were specially designed to burn a variety of grades of coal, including the cheapest Indian fuel.

Never adopting innovations unless they improved the expectations of profit over the whole range of trades in which their ships were engaged, Harrisons paid much attention to improvements in furnace design and the performance of the reciprocating engine in the inter-war era. Thus their *Settler* of 1939, the last ship delivered before the war, attained nearly 17 knots on trials from a triple expansion engine exhausting into a Bauer-Wach turbine, taking superheated steam from coal-fired, double-ended Scotch boilers.

In 1928 Harrisons experimented with mechanical stoking arrangements aboard their *Musician.* Small coal (slack or duff) was bunkered, pulverised aboard ship and blown into the boiler furnaces. Next year the new *Recorder* was fitted for pulverised fuel before entering service.

Unfortunately, savings forecast in bunkering time, trimming and handling costs were outweighed by larger diseconomies. Few ports overseas could supply suitable coal in sufficient quantities. Time was lost, even in the home port, Liverpool, because of a shortage of suitable berths for the sort of bunkering operations required. Finally the mechanical stoking arrangements generated excessive noise and dirt.

In 'Shipping Enterprise and Management' by Professor F. E. Hyde, Professor J. R. Harris, in a special contribution notes that Harrisons were soon concerned about the limited flexibility of routing a vessel using pulverised fuel. In the managers' report for 1931 it was stated: 'The powdered coal experiment has proved that if a vessel fitted with appropriate machinery can be run between two given points regularly, a considerable saving might be effected.' However, the limitations which have been noted brought the experiment to an end.

A consideration to be borne in mind when assessing the comparative merits of different types of mechanical propulsion is that, even on very basic calculations, oil provides a 50 per cent increase in heat value for the same bunker space over coal and so leaves more room for cargo. When used aboard a diesel-engined ship, one ton of oil does the same amount of work as two tons of oil or three tons of coal employed to fire conventional steam boilers.

ALAN McCLELLAND, 33 Montclair Drive, Mossley Hill, Liverpool L18 0HB

Harrison's *Musician* (4,663/1919), subject of experiments with mechanical stoking in the late 1920s. The former Rankin and Gilnour *Saint Bede, Musician* was sold in 1938 and lasted until 1961. *[J. and M. Clarkson]*

Cable compressors and losing the *Highcliffe*

In issue 19 of *Record* I wonder if readers noted an interesting feature on the collier *Fireside* (page 184)? She has a pair of cable compressors immediately aft, and in line with the winch barrels, of the two winches at the stem.

When moored at the coal chutes, wire cables were led through the compressors directly to the winches, and by these means the ship could be moved ahead or astern to suit the loading spout. On the forecastle the head wire was led through the outboard compressor and a back spring wire through the inboard compressor, this was repeated aft.

The use of the cable compressors to clamp the mooring wires in this manner reduced greatly the labour required to handle mooring wires on and off the bollards, one man on the forecastle and one aft could carry out the movements, and also avoided need to use the engines.

The accompanying photograph is of a cable compressor fitted on the *Aberthaw Fisher*.

The second *Highcliffe* (*Record* 19, page 153) actually stranded on Forewick Holm, which is close to Papa Stour island in St. Magnus Bay, which is some 40 miles north, and could not be classed as near Fitful Head. Her Captain, James Henderson, lived in Newcastle-upon-Tyne, but belonged originally to Reawick in Shetland. The Aith lifeboat rescued the 28 crew. *Highcliffe* stranded in dense fog, and as a schoolboy in Burra Isle, Shetland, I can remember the local fishing boats from my village going to help in the rescue.

JAMES POTTINGER, 1 Jesmond Circle, Bridge of Don, Aberdeen AB22 8WX

SOURCES AND ACKNOWLEDGEMENTS

Photographs are from the collection of John Clarkson unless otherwise credited. We thank all who gave permission for their photographs to be used, and for help in finding photographs we are particularly grateful to Tony Smith, Jim McFaul and David Whiteside of the World Ship Photo Library; to Ian Farquhar, Bill Laxon, Peter Newall, Ivor Rooke, William Schell, George Scott; to David Hodge and Bob Todd of the National Maritime Museum; Dr. David Jenkins of the National Museums and Galleries of Wales; and other museums and institutions listed.

Research sources have included the *Registers* of William Schell and Tony Starke, *Lloyd's Register, Lloyd's Confidential Index, Lloyd's War Losses, Mercantile Navy Lists,* and *Marine News.* Use of the facilities of the World Ship Society's Central Record, the Guildhall Library, the Public Record Office and Lloyd's Register of Shipping are gratefully acknowledged. Particular thanks also to William Schell and John Bartlett for various information, to Heather Fenton for editorial and indexing work, and to Marion Clarkson for accountancy services.

Sources and acknowledgements from several articles in *Record* 19 have been held over until this issue because of lack of space.

Houlder's Post-war Granges

The articles were based on the author's personal recollections, plus company records, and drawing office note books. In addition, the following were consulted:
W.H. Mitchell and L.A. Sawyer *The Oceans, the Forts and the Parks* Sea Breezes, Liverpool
David Burrell *The Centenary History of Furness, Withy and Company Ltd., 1891-1991* World Ship Society, Kendal, 1992.

The Nile Steamship Co. Ltd.

In addition to those listed above, sources include Lithgow Archives (University of Glasgow), Sir William Lithgow, J.E. Boyd, Lord Mackay of Clashfern, David Asprey, Companies House (Edinburgh), National Maritime Museum (Greenwich), 3i plc and Erling D. Naess *Autobiography of a Shipping Man.*

John Bowes: the first bulk carrier?

The *John Bowes* has been well written up, although authors disagree about important details such as her ballast arrangements. It is remarkable, however, that some otherwise worthy books do not mention the ship at all. The strangest omission is in *The Advent of Steam: The Merchant Steamship before 1900*, edited by Basil Greenhill in the Conway's History of the Ship series. Whilst its august academic contributors catalogue improvements in performance and power, they give ships carrying bulk commodities - the single largest segment of the world's trade - virtually no mention. Sources used were:

Dick Keys and Ken Smith *Steamers at the Staiths: Steam Colliers of the North East 1841-1945* Tyne Bridge Publishing, Newcastle, 2000
Dick Keys and Ken Smith *Black Diamonds by Sea: North East Sailing Colliers 1780-1880* Newcastle Libraries and Information Service, Newcastle, 1998
J.A. MacRae and C.V. Waine *The Steam Collier Fleets* Waine Research Publications, Albrighton, 1990
E.E Allen 'On the Comparative Cost of Transit by Steam and Sailing Colliers, and on the Different Methods of Ballasting.' *Proceedings of the Institute of Civil Engineers* XIV (1854-5), 318-73
C.M Palmer 'On the Construction of Iron Ships and the Progress of Iron Shipbuilding on the Tyne, Wear and Tees.' *Report of the British Association for the Advancement of Science for 1863* 694-701
F.C Bowen (writing as FCB) 'Ships that made History: V The *John Bowes'*. *Shipbuilding and Shipping Record* 30th September 1937, 421-2
David Bell 'Palmer's shipyard and the old John Bowes.' *Sea Breezes* April 1998, 316-319
Crew agreements, class BT 98, in the Pubic Record Office, London.

British liner - Greek tramp

Transaction details have been compiled using the closed ships' registers at the Public Record Office (BT110) and reports in the British shipping periodical *Fairplay.* Supplementary information has come from sources cited above plus Duncan Haws' Merchant Fleets series and from the following:
David Burrell *The Centenary History of Furness, Withy and Company Ltd., 1891-1991* World Ship Society, Kendal, 1992
James E. Cowden and John O.C. Duffy *The Elder Dempster Fleet History, 1852-1985.* Mallett and Bell, London, 1986
Edwin Green and Michael Moss *A Business of National Importance: The Royal Mail Shipping Group, 1902-1937.* Methuen, London, 1982
Gelina Harlaftis *A History of Greek-Owned Shipping. The Making of an International Tramp Fleet, 1830 to the Present Day* Routledge, London, 1996
Roger Jordan *The World's Merchant Fleets, 1939* Conway, London, 1999
Manolis E. Kulukundis *Ships Loved and Painted* Krikos, London, 1977
Andreas G. Lemos *The Greeks and the Sea. A Peoples' Seafaring Achievements from Ancient Times to the Present Day* Cassell, London, 1976
Jürgen Rohwer *Axis Submarine Successes 1939-1945.* Patrick Stephens, Cambridge, 1983
Jürgen Rohwer *Allied Submarine Attacks of World War Two.* Greenhill, London, 1997
P.M. Heaton *Lamport & Holt* Heaton, Pontypool, 1986
W.H. Mitchell and L.A. Sawyer *British Standard Ships of World War 1* Sea Breezes, Liverpool, 1968
Peter Newall *Union-Castle Line A Fleet History,* Carmania, London, 1999.

Every picture tells a story

Basil Lubbock writes at length about the *Berean* and Walker's fleet in *The Colonial Clippers* Brown, Son and Ferguson, Ltd., Glasgow, 1948, 153-60. Frank C. Bowen provides a shorter account in *Sailing Ships of the London River* Sampson Low, Marston and Co., Ltd., London, n.d. (c.1930), 89-95.

Irish port and harbour scenes

Thanks to Grainne Mac Lochlainn of the National Photograph Archive, National Library of Ireland. The author has drawn on information from two books, Kieran Hickey *The Light of Other Days* (Allen Lane, 1973) which has a very good account of Lawrence and French, but is let down by indifferent reproduction of the photographs; and Patrick Flanagan *Transport in Ireland 1880 - 1910* (Transport Research Associates, Dublin, 1969) which in contrast reproduces the Lawrence photographs wonderfully well.

Bank engines (*Record* 19)

The brief notes on Harland and Wolff were drawn from Michael Moss and John R. Hume *Shipbuilders to the World; 125 Years of Harland and Wolff, Belfast 1861-1986* Blackstaff Press, Belfast and Wolfsboro, New Hampshire, 1986. Ian Stewart *British Tramps and their Peacetime Contribution to World Shipping History* Ian Stewart Marine Publications, 1997, provides an excellent short account of the development of Doxford, and its demise amidst the decline of British shipbuilding. The drawing of the Doxford J-type engine is from *The Motor Ship' Reference Book, 21st Edition,* Temple Press Books Ltd., London, 1965. David Aris, former Fitting Out Manager for Doxfords, kindly provided additional information on these engines.

IRISH PORT AND HARBOUR SCENES:
THE LAWRENCE COLLECTION
Part 1
Ian Wilson

This is a selection of views from the period 1890 to 1910 drawn from the vast collection of the William Lawrence firm, housed now in the National Library of Ireland, Dublin. It is intended to be a representative sample of ports and harbours, large and small, and there are scores, indeed probably hundreds, more high quality photographs of equal maritime interest. Some of this selection are being published for the first time; some others appeared only in the very scarce book 'Transport in Ireland 1880 - 1910', published in 1969. Quite apart from the detail that is of interest to maritime historians, most of the photographs can be enjoyed for their sheer aesthetic beauty. Can there be many more impressive views of a ship in an Irish harbour than the one of the handsome steam coaster at Westport Quay, with Croaghpatrick mountain looming beyond? Most of these views will have been the work of one man, Robert French, of whom the Irish author and film-maker Kieran Hickey has said, '...his talent for finding the right angle and the right timing is remarkable, as is the completeness of each picture - every relevant thing within it positioned accurately ... he was aware of and prepared for that fraction of a second in which a commonplace image is transformed into a precise and living one.'

The Lawrence Collection
In 1943, an auction took place in Dublin. A Mr. William Lawrence junior was closing down his long-established family toy and fancy goods emporium. The auctioneer's notice advertised the shop's fittings and included '...a large quantity of photographic negatives, for which Messrs. Lawrence were famous.' Dublin in wartime - or 'the emergency' - was drab and needy. A scarcity of glass had resulted in another studio's glass negatives being bought for use in greenhouses. The Lawrence archive could easily have been destroyed had it not been for railway historian Kevin Murray, who persuaded the National Library of its worth. For £300, the Library acquired an astounding 40,000 negatives. It must be one of the best decisions the Library ever made, for it is impossible to do justice in words to the magnificence and historical value of the Lawrence collection.

William Lawrence senior (1840- 1932) was, in the early part of his career, one of the many progressive portrait photographers to be found in all big European cities. His photographic business was helped by the fact that the toy shop was the best-known in Dublin, and by the mid-1860s stereoscopic scenic views were being taken, too. But Lawrence was not the actual photographer. As Kieran Hickey puts it in his Lawrence selection 'The Light of Other Days' (Allen Lane, 1973) '...prosperous Victorian businessmen were not likely to lower themselves to their

workmen, even in a craft as comparatively arcane as photography.' His chief outdoor photographer was Robert French (1841-1917) and most of the views seen here will undoubtedly have been taken by French.

Eastman's dry-plate negative was a major step forward in photography in the 1870s. No longer had outdoor photographers to carry developing materials around with them. All French needed was his camera, a tripod and a supply of glass plates. For thirty years, a methodical and comprehensive coverage of Irish scenes was undertaken. Once out-of-date (for example, with the coming of trams and then motor cars) street scenes were conscientiously replaced. French was given free rein to photograph Ireland. Lawrence would book his rail ticket and hotel, and often delegate one of his children to help carry the equipment! On return to Dublin, the negatives would be printed, to be sold as framed pictures, prints and magic lantern slides; to illustrate guides and travel books; as cigarette cards (Gallaher's issued 600 views) and, of course for picture postcards. The craze for postcards between 1902 and 1914 resulted in untold millions being produced and this enormous new outlet benefited the Lawrence firm greatly. At just this time, too, Ireland was opening up for tourism with new hotels, steamship and road services, exemplified in some of the scenes published here.

Lawrence became one of Dublin's leading businessmen, but by 1912 both he and French were over 70, and in September of that year a weary French complained in a letter home that he had been obliged to travel from the south-west to the north-east of the island on assignments. Output slowed down. The cataloguing system became less scrupulous. In 1914 French retired. At his farewell, he was presented with a framed reproduction of one of his own photographs. Other events that year, and the political turbulence in Ireland until 1922, altered the mood of the country. The Lawrence toy shop, opposite the GPO, was burned and looted in the Easter Rising in 1916. The firm's records were lost but the negatives, stored elsewhere, mercifully survived.

After the National Library acquired the collection, a haphazard cataloguing system was introduced, and it has taken many years for this to be superceded effectively. In a very different Dublin to the one Lawrence knew - and to the Dublin of 1943 - the Lawrence Collection is now housed in the superb new National Photographic Archive in the attractive, regenerated Temple Bar area on the south bank of the Liffey. The building incorporates a substantial air-conditioned storage area, together with darkrooms, a conservation area, reading room, exhibition gallery, and retail space. Inquiries should be addressed to the National Photographic Archive, Meeting House Square, Dublin 2.

Sligo
On the south bank of the Garavogue River, the mile-long quays are today largely derelict, except for an active berth at the extreme seaward end. Depicted here, though, is a wide variety of shipping at what used to be an important port. The Laird Line and Sligo Steam Navigation Company carried passengers to Glasgow and Liverpool respectively, but mostly we see cargo vessels, captured looking upstream. The large steamer is the *Heathmore* of W. Johnston and Co., Liverpool, built at the forgotten yard of J. Key and Sons, Kinghorn, Fife, in 1883. The unusual steamer alongside her is probably one of the lighters regularly needed to attend vessels in Sligo Bay before they could proceed past the famous 'Metal Man' marker off Rosses Point, and into the river. The small steamer in the foreground could well be the *Tartar*, which for over forty years from 1899 served the small communities in areas of poor roads west of Sligo, terminating at remote Belmullet, County Mayo. [National Library of Ireland CAB 5616]

Westport, County Mayo.

The Laird Line's west of Ireland service extended on alternate weeks from Sligo to Ballina and Westport, both in County Mayo. The long tidal quay here was about sixteen miles from the open sea, reached through the islands of Clew Bay, in the shadow of Croaghpatrick, on which Saint Patrick is reputed to have performed his banishment of Ireland's snakes! In this stunning setting, the Lawrence photographer has depicted a typical three-masted steam coaster of the 1900 era. She appears to be unloading bagged flour with her steam winches into horse-drawn carts. A Galway hooker lies upstream. These ubiquitous craft carried turf and other cargoes around the indented Galway and Mayo coastline and out to the islands under sail until the early 1970s. Westport town, more than a mile away, is now a tourist honeypot, but coasters occasionally still call as do small vessels engaged in the extensive modern fish-farming business. *[National Library of Ireland IMP 1265]*

Kilrush, County Clare

Closer to the town of Kilrush than its deep-water Cappagh Quay - in fact at the foot of Main Street - was Merchants' Quay. Kilrush is near the mouth of the huge Shannon estuary, and these small smacks are most likely estuarial traders, such as the *Maria* of Limerick (right). She has been visited by a swarm of local boys, one standing barefoot on her damaged bulwark. It was the custom in small Irish ports for people to invite themselves aboard visiting vessels. These craft do not have the characteristic 'tumblehome' (bulging hull shape) or raked rudder of the Galway hooker, and some defy easy classification. A siding from the narrow-gauge West Clare Railway ran down Merchants' Quay. Its eccentric ways were celebrated in the Percy French song 'Are Ye Right There Michael!' Today the tidal creek leads to new lock gates and Kilrush Creek Marina. Happily, a sailing ship returned to the Merchants' Quay area when the Irish sail-training brigantine *Asgard II* docked. The excellent website www.kilrushcreekmarina.ie has photographs of this, plenty on the Shannon estuary, and links to sites related to the heritage town of Kilrush - where even the railway is being restored!

[National Library of Ireland R4259]

QUAYS. KILRUSH. 4259. W.L.

Cappagh Quay, Kilrush

A mile or so seawards from the tidal Merchants' Quay creek lies the substantial Cappagh Quay, which had a good depth of water and a connection to the West Clare Railway. Passengers heading for the resort of Kilkee were able to sail the 35 miles from Limerick, via intermediate piers, to Cappagh Quay and board the grandly-named 'Steamship Express'. In this carefully composed view, we see the paddlers *Mermaid* (left) and *Shannon*, both owned by the Waterford Steamship Company. Formerly the Clyde steamer *Largs*, built in 1864, the *Mermaid* worked on the estuary from 1875 until 1903, while the *Shannon*, built in Belfast in 1892, spent her career here until the route closed during the First World War. The handsome ketch is named *Mildred*. Cargoes of Scandinavian timber still arrive at Cappagh Quay, and, while the paddle steamers are long gone, a scenic 20-minute car ferry crossing of the estuary can be enjoyed from nearby Killimer to Tarbet on the south shore. *[National Library of Ireland R4252]*

CAPPAGH PIER. KILRUSH. 4252. W.L.

Bangor, County Down

The iron paddler *Erin*, a similar Clyde-built steamer to the *Mermaid*, is pictured arriving at Bangor on one of her regular sailings from Belfast. Unlike the Shannon routes, which were a vital transport artery in the estuary, the Belfast Lough service was a summer-only facility for passengers who had the choice of taking a train. But the 'Bangor boat' was a much-loved institution from 1852 until 1915, as city dwellers escaped to the seaside or office workers travelled to work in Belfast enjoying the benefit of sea air. Thereafter, a proper timetabled service only operated in 1923 and 1924, with the former Blackpool paddler *Greyhound*, although occasional excursions were popular up to the Second World War. The *Erin* and her similar consort *Bangor Castle* ran in tandem for over 20 years until 1894 for Moore Brothers. Trips to other ports such as Larne and Donaghadee were offered. However, the company probably over-reached themselves in 1887, with the delivery of the much larger, powerful steel paddler *Clandeboye*, which took day trips as far as Ayr. After two seasons, and no doubt a huge amount of coal, she was sold to DFDS for their Copenhagen to Malmo service. Here a crew member prepares the heaving line as excursionists crowd to the bows to see the delights of the seaside approaching. At the time of writing, two new catamarans have arrived in Belfast for a firm intending to re-open the route for commuters. *[National Library of Ireland R2457]*

BANGOR STEAMER 2457 W.L..

Youghal, County Cork

Lawrence's photographs capture an Ireland just opening up to tourism. In this superb study, excursionists are joining the paddler *Dartmouth Castle* for the scenic sixteen-mile voyage up the River Blackwater to Cappoquin. This photograph can confidently be dated 1907, the steamer's first season after her purchase that June from the River Dart, as for the next season she appeared with a shorter funnel, white hull and no mainmast. Her owners were Michael Kennedy of Youghal and Richard Keane of Cappoquin, who founded the evocatively named Youghal and Blackwater Tourist Steamship Co. Ltd. Close examination of this photograph shows that the steamer needed a floating pontoon, a small hulk, the gangplank being a structure not likely to meet modern Health and Safety criteria! One of the ladies in Edwardian finery holds on to her hat as she decides whether to board. At the commercial quay to seawards lies a large sailing vessel. Youghal, a historic and attractive small town, is still an active port which gave a tremendous welcome to the preserved West Country schooner *Kathleen and May* when she arrived from Bideford on her return to Irish waters after many decades, in August 2001. The sailings by the *Dartmouth Castle*, built by Harvey of Hayle in 1885, ceased in 1913. [*National Library of Ireland R9611*]

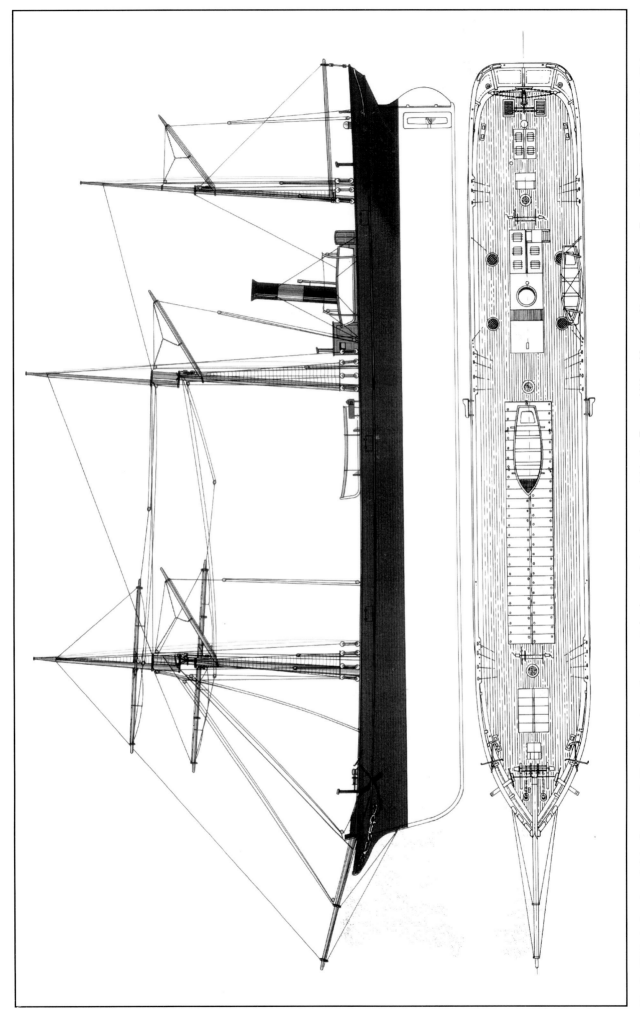

Charles Waine's drawing of *John Bowes* as built and rigged as a three-masted schooner is based on a model in the Tyne and Wear Museum, Newcastle-upon-Tyne. Note the 60-foot hatch which, thanks to the strength of her iron hull, could be considerably bigger than that of a contemporary wooden sailing collier, facilitating loading and discharge. *[Courtesy Dr Charles Waine]*

JOHN BOWES: THE FIRST BULK CARRIER?
Roy Fenton

July 2002 sees the 150th anniversary of one of the most important ships ever built. The *John Bowes*, which was completed at Jarrow in July 1852, was not merely the forerunner of the large fleet of steam colliers which was to serve the immense east coast coal trade, although this was achievement enough. This article will argue that she was the pioneer of the vessels which carry much of today's world trade in relatively-low value commodities, the bulk carrier.

Origins and antecedents

Since the middle ages London had obtained most of its fuel from the coalfields of Durham and Northumberland. A fleet of small sailing colliers - snows, brigs, brigantines and schooners - developed to serve this trade, and that from the north east to other harbours around the south and east coasts of the United Kingdom. The importance of this coal trade can be judged from the numbers of vessels involved: Keys and Smith report that in 1830 there were over 11,000 sailings from the Tyne alone, and calculate that, from 1830 until the end of the sailing trade, just under 3,000 different sailing colliers were owned on Tyneside. To these must be added perhaps an equal number owned on the Wear, in London and other ports.

This 'sea coal' trade grew almost continually until the middle of the nineteenth century. By then the rail network was extensive and railways had become both mechanically and commercially efficient enough to offer a strong challenge to coastal sail for the carriage of coal. For the coal owners of the north east, the threat was particularly severe, as coal from the more-recently developed fields in the east midlands and Yorkshire could now compete for the London market. The disadvantages of the sailing collier which carried coal from the Tyne and Wear now became important. Unloading was slow, impeded by small hatches necessary on a wooden vessel and by their spars and rigging, and not helped by restrictive practices amongst the coal whippers who discharged the colliers. Vagaries of the weather made voyage times unpredictable, which meant large fluctuations in price on the London market as whole fleets of colliers were either wind-bound and caused a coal famine, or arrived together to offer a glut.

By the mid 19th century, iron-hulled steamers had become well established in the coastal and short-sea liner trades. Speed and predictability of sailing and arrival times were particularly important in these trades which were predominantly carrying passengers, perishable goods such

Wooden sailing colliers dominated the carriage of north east coal before the screw colliers were developed, and continued to be built in some numbers. The 177-ton brig *Ebenezer* was built at Kingston (better known as Shoreham), Sussex in 1860. The competition from screw colliers, over 50 of which were in service by the year *Ebenezer* was built, undoubtedly encouraged their builders to make the sailing collier more efficient, although this meant harder work for their crews. During the 1890s *Ebenezer* was part of the fleet of Stephenson Clarke who were operating sail and steam colliers side by side.

In what seems a very one-sided contest, *Ebenezer* was captured by a German submarine north west of Dieppe on 25th July 1917 and sunk by explosive charges. *[National Maritime Museum P2726]*

as foodstuffs or time-sensitive items such as mail. However, the bulk trades remained largely invulnerable to steam, even after the development of the screw in the late 1830s meant that engines could be placed aft, maximising the hold space for a bulky cargo. At least five unsuccessful or inconclusive experiments with iron-hulled screw colliers are documented in the 1840s. The *Bedlington* of 1841 was essentially a rail-wagon ferry built to overcome local difficulties in the coal trade out of Blyth. She ventured only as far as Shields and cost so much to repair after her frequent groundings that her use was abandoned after five years, her owners turning to rail transport. The *Q.E.D.* of 1844 is reported to have had a double bottom arranged to give tanks for water ballast, but she had her engines removed after little more than a year. The *Experiment* of 1845 is said to have been a collier but actually carried general cargo and passengers between Sunderland and London until her loss in 1848. The *Conside* of 1847 and the *Collier* of 1849 were evidently conceived as colliers but were placed into regular liner trades immediately on completion, the *Conside* between Leith and Hamburg and *Collier* on the English Channel. *Conside* was lost in 1852, but *Collier* survived until 1914, in the latter part of her long life undoubtedly carrying the cargo for which she had been named.

The embryo screw collier had considerable disadvantages to overcome. It cost much more to build than a sailing ship of equivalent capacity, and repairs to iron hull and machinery needed particular and expensive skills. With its boiler's voracious appetite for fuel and the inefficiency of its low-pressure steam engines it cost much more to run. Added to this was the expense of providing firemen and engineers who were in addition to a full deck crew, as sail was still carried. The steamer's advantages were that it could make voyages of a predictable duration, and - most importantly - could make significantly more of them in a given time than a sailing collier. But even then practices in the coal trade limited the application of the screw collier. A

'turn system' was applied in many ports so that a vessel was loaded or unloaded strictly according to the order in which it arrived. Standing idle for days or weeks in a congested port was death to the steamer with its much higher capital and running costs. The problem was compounded in the London coal trade by the need to queue to take on chalk or shingle ballast for the northbound voyage, and to unload it on arrival in the Tyne or Wear.

The *John Bowes'* success

In the early 1850s Charles Mark Palmer bought an existing yard at Jarrow. Shipyards on the Tyne and Wear had been building in iron since 1842, but Palmer felt they had made little progress. He noted that the vessels most in demand were colliers, but that no-one had thought of applying iron to these. His first completion was the iron tug *Northumbria*, launched without ceremony in 1851, but it is clear that his ambition was for the yard to build screw colliers. His stated aim with the *John Bowes* was to design a screw steamer of the greatest possible capacity with engines just sufficiently powerful to ensure regularity of service, with a speed of nine knots. Palmer combined engineering courage (some contemporaries called it rashness) with an appreciation of the importance of good publicity. The launch of *John Bowes* on 30th June 1852 and the subsequent dinner and dance was attended by many important figures from local industry and commerce, but perhaps Palmer's biggest coup was to have the 'Illustrated London News' reproduce an illustration of the launch. Built of Derwent iron, with decks of teak, *John Bowes* had a two-cylinder steam engine built by Robert Stephenson and Co., the railway and marine engineers. She had a large hatch to serve her 60-foot hold.

In March 1852 Palmer had been influential in setting up the General Iron Screw Collier Company Limited, with a massive nominal capital of £250,000 in £5 shares. It seems likely that this company would have financed the *John Bowes*, but not for the first time the

The only one of *John Bowes'* collier predecessors which survived long enough to be photographed, although undoubtedly much modified, was *Collier*. The name certainly hints that she was destined for the coal trade, but her earliest crew agreements show that she was employed exclusively between Shoreham in Sussex and the Channel Isles, making 35 voyages each year. From the absence of coal mines in Sussex one would conclude that she was carrying general cargo. From 1878 *Collier* was owned continuously by the Pockett family of Swansea and later Bristol, who adopted the stirring title Pockett's Bristol Channel Steam Packet Co. Ltd. On 28th January 1914 she was wrecked in fog on Rockham Shoal, Mortehoe and was beached near Bull Point Lighthouse whilst on a ballast voyage from Milford to Avonmouth. *[Author's collection]*

engineers moved faster than accountants and solicitors, so that the collier was floated well before the company, which was not completely registered until September 1852. Members of the Palmer family took a total of 22 shares in her, the rest of the finance being from a businessman in Manchester and engineer James MacConnell who worked for the London and North Western Railway at Wolverton. The collier was named in honour of John Bowes, Sheriff of the County and - more significantly - an important local coal owner, of the Marley Hill Coal Company, although he never had a financial interest in the ship. In the registration papers of the General Iron Screw Collier Company, Palmer describes himself as a coal owner, and it has been suggested that he was an investor in Bowes' mines. But if so why did Palmer need to flatter Bowes by giving his name to the collier? It seems most likely that Palmer had little financial interest in Bowes' mines and that the name of the new collier was intended to influence him to use her to ship Marley Hill coal.

John Bowes' successful first voyage has been widely described, again largely because of Palmer's flair for publicity and the willingness of the 'Illustrated London News' to report her arrival on the Thames. Somewhat embarrassingly for Tyneside, she seems to have loaded at Sunderland, where her first crew agreement was signed on 29th July 1852, just five days after she had been first registered at Newcastle. From the Wear she took just 48 hours to reach the Thames, 24 hours to discharge, and 48 hours to return northwards, arriving back on the Tyne on 3rd August. Palmer claimed that, by delivering 650 tons of coal in five days, *John Bowes* had done the equivalent of a month's work by two average sailing colliers.

Crew agreements for her first year in service confirm that *John Bowes* consistently made regular and speedy round trips, although her continuing performance was not as good as that achieved on her first voyage. She completed 14 round voyages from the end of July to the end of December, an average of 11 days per round trip. Crew agreements quote the dates for leaving the Tyne and arriving back there, and these are between five and eight days apart. Turnround times on the Tyne are not always very smart, and vary from one day to six.

Water ballast: the key innovation

John Bowes' initial five-day round trip clearly represented a special effort to prove the advantages of screw colliers. Her later and generally poorer performance strongly suggests that unloading of her first cargo of coal must have been skilfully organised to avoid delaying her, and so must have been the loading of solid ballast for her return voyage. Although water ballast had been tried previously, possibly by the *Q.E.D.*, it is

The depiction of the launch of *John Bowes* in the 'Illustrated London News'. The artist has got the positions of her masts approximately correct, and the launch was certainly well attended. But the significance of the illustration is in showing how Palmer was aware of the importance of publicity for the products of his shipyard, an awareness which certainly paid off in repeat orders.

clear that *John Bowes* was not built with the capability to use water ballast, as some authors have implied. However, Palmer was clearly concerned about the delays inherent in loading and unloading chalk or sand ballast. He is said to have placed barrels in the hold of the *John Bowes* which could be filled with water and which, when she approached the Tyne, were emptied into the bilges, from where the pump emptied it overside. This was a very cumbersome method of ballasting, as the barrels had to be destroyed each voyage. There is considerable contradiction in the published literature about the exact ballast arrangements adopted for the *John Bowes,* probably explained by Palmer's continual experimenting with her; he later noted that several methods of ballasting had been tried. What eventually proved successful - and was undoubtedly the innovation which made steam colliers and their successors economically viable - were shallow tanks for water ballast fitted along the ship's bottom. These double-bottom tanks had the further advantage of adding strength to the hull. They became known as McIntyre tanks after their inventor, who Palmer had engaged from Clydeside in May 1852. John McIntyre's letter of appointment actually mentions an idea for water tanks, so the idea was in the air before *John Bowes* was completed. Again, there is uncertainty whether the McIntyre tanks were actually tried first in *John Bowes* (which would have involved extensive rebuilding), or were first built into the new collier *Samuel Laing* (yard number 21, 563/1854). McIntyre is one of the unsung heroes of naval architecture, who deserves better recognition for his vital contribution to cargo ship design, although it is fitting that a later Palmer collier was named after him: yard number 127 was launched as *John McIntyre* on 15th July 1863.

Water ballast solved just one of the problems faced by the steam collier. According to the Coal Turn Act, she still had to wait her turn to be loaded or unloaded. The *John Bowes* herself was the subject of litigation brought by a sailing ship owner. After loading Tyne coal during 1853, her place under the coal spouts was taken by the sailing collier *William*. When only part of the *William's* coal cargo had been loaded, the *John Bowes* returned, and the sailing ship was

hauled off to make way for her. The *Williams'* owners brought a successful action under the Coal Turn Act. The coal owners' response was to build staithes that were reserved for loading steamers. On the Thames, much effort was put into mechanising unloading. The most notable development was the introduction in 1862 of William Cory's *Atlas,* a pontoon equipped with steam cranes which could simultaneously unload the cargoes of two colliers into barges. The long-term solution to the steamer owners' difficulties came with the repeal of the Coal Turn Act in 1865.

The collier multiplies

Although her initial lack of water ballast tanks reduces somewhat the significance of *John Bowes* as a pioneer, she indisputably demonstrated that an iron-hulled, steam-driven vessel could work economically in the bulk trades. This is shown by how quickly her design was multiplied. Palmer's yard launched *William Hutt* (530/1852) in December 1952, but the pace of launches at Jarrow then quickened considerably, presumably because extra launching ways were laid down, as three ships entered the water on 13th

August 1853, including the colliers *Jarrow* (yard number 8; 531/1853) and *Marley Hill* (yard number 10; 508/1853), the latter name another nod in the direction of John Bowes.

John Bowes' performance was quickly bettered. *Jarrow* is recorded as making 29 voyages in 1854, her first complete year in service. However, an even more impressive performance was noted for the big collier *James Dixon* (yard number 88; 1,053/1859). Palmer claimed she made 57 voyages to London in 1860, and the voyages recorded in her crew agreements for that year are consistent with this level of performance.

With completions at other yards, including that of John Scott Russell on the Thames, around 70 steam colliers were built in the five years following the completion of the *John Bowes.* Gradually the steam collier fleet began to recapture the coal trade from the railways. Towards the middle of the 1870s, the amount of coal shipped coastwise from the Tyne, Wear and Tees (most of which went to London) began to rise again, having been in slow decline for several decades. By 1898 the total tonnage of coal brought to London by sea again exceeded that brought by rail, an

Opposite is the earlier of the two known photographs of *John Bowes* under her original name. She still has a rudimentary bowsprit and the suggestion of a clipper bow, although the staging suggests this may soon be altered. *[Newcastle-upon-Tyne City Libraries and Arts]*

Right is the better-known photograph of *John Bowes*, taken after her rig had been reduced, her bowsprit removed and the bow straightened. The backdrop is presumably Palmer's yard. *[National Maritime Museum A317]*

Named after the inventor of double-bottom water ballast tanks, *John McIntyre* demonstrates a virtue of the double-bottom: an ability to survive strandings (middle). The 1863-built collier has a similar rig to the *John Bowes* (note the sails, brailed to her masts), but with the bridge moved amidships - an arrangement widely adopted for engines-aft colliers. *John McIntyre* survived until May 1910 when a collision in the Thames and subsequent beaching at Plaistow led to her sale to Dutch shipbreakers. *[Author's collection]*

The problem of rapid and efficient unloading of screw colliers on the crowded Thames was successfully addressed by William Cory who operated a series of pontoons moored in the tideway, each carrying a battery of steam cranes to discharge the coal into lighters. Below is *Atlas No. 3* with Cory's Sunderland-built *Surf* (1,597/1896) alongside. *[Author's collection]*

achievement that is entirely to the credit of the steam collier and those like Charles Palmer who put their faith and their money into them.

The *John Bowes* in service

Notwithstanding the arrival of more efficient colliers, *John Bowes* continued to work in the east coast coal trade under Palmer's ownership for the best part of 20 years. On occasion, she diverted to Port Mulgrave in North Yorkshire, where she would load iron ore from Palmer's own workings for delivery to their furnaces at Jarrow. Like many other colliers, *John Bowes* was requisitioned to take stores out to the Crimean War once the War Office's incompetence in providing sufficient supplies for the army became fully apparent. She left London on 10th December 1854 for a voyage which ended at Balaclava, not returning until July 1855. She was to make one other similar voyage to the Black Sea, with calls at Malta, Constantinople, Scutari, Kertch and Genoa, before returning to Portsmouth. Her continuing life in the coal trade, although more routine, was certainly not without incident, and in 'Steamers at the Staithes' Dick Keys and Ken Smith faithfully chronicle the many collisions and other mishaps in which she was involved.

Palmers re-engined *John Bowes* in 1862. It is unlikely that her original machinery was worn out, but more probably her owners recognised the economies that could be achieved with more efficient machinery, as she was fitted with a two-cylinder compound engine made on the Clyde. The advantages of compounding in improving efficiency and reducing coal consumption (and with it the need for firemen) had been appreciated for at least ten years, and was tried in the *Brandon* of 1854, but it had not been widely applied. Palmers were in the van once again, as Alfred Holt's well-documented experiments with compounding did not start until his *Cleator* was re-engined in 1863.

In 1873 Palmers sold *John Bowes,* retaining a fleet of small coasters for their Port Mulgrave ironstone trade. At a modest 150 feet, *John Bowes* was now comparatively small for the east coast trade: the average length of steam colliers was now around 180 feet. Nevertheless, she settled down to an even longer spell of uninterrupted trading for Barnett Brothers of London. The Barnetts were shipbrokers, and they quickly sold most of the 64 shares in *John Bowes* to other small investors, remaining as managing owners with a small shareholding that varied from year to year. She remained in the east coast coal trade, and Barnetts were prepared to invest money in her. In 1883 she was given a new engine, the third she had carried, and had alterations to her mast, engines and hull in 1886.

In 1896, after 23 years with Barnetts, *John Bowes* was sold to Dublin, and now traded on the Irish Sea. But a further accident put her new owners into financial straits. She was sold by order of the Admiralty Marshall to a London shipbroker, and was resold to the first of a series of overseas owners. As *Spec* and then *Transit* she ran for Norwegian and later Swedish operators. On occasion she still visited the Tyne where she was photographed passing her birthplace at Palmers' yard. In 1908 her 56-year old hull and 25-year old engines could still fetch the equivalent of £2,000, the figure at which she is reported sold to Spanish owners as *Carolina*. She was now in the iron ore trade out of Bilbao and under the further names *Valentin Fierro* (see photographs) and *Villa Selgas,* she survived until foundering during a coastal voyage in November 1933, although fortunately without loss of life.

The *John Bowes* inheritance: a hypothesis

Colliers grew quickly in size, and the ambitions and horizons of their owners grew with them, so that very quickly they were voyaging beyond London and indeed beyond the east coast coal trade. Of course, it was not an enormous step to carry coal from the Tyne or Wear to ports on the other side of the North Sea, notably Hamburg, and north round the tip of Denmark into the Baltic. Estimates based on crew agreements for steam colliers in the decade to 1860 suggest that the vessels were spending 40% of their time outside the strictly coastal trade. This is an average: some vessels did much more foreign-going, others less. During her first year in service, the Palmers'-built *Hutton Chaytor* (yard number 34; 529/1855) was exclusively voyaging between Hartlepool and London. Yet by 1858 she was hardly in the coal trade at all. Two voyages were made into the Mediterranean, and one to the Baltic, terminating at Cronstadt. Only in October does she return to the coal trade, making two voyages from Sunderland to London. In 1860, all *Hutton Chaytor's* voyages were foreign-going, indeed beyond the Home Trade Limits. What is perplexing is that no voyages originate in the coal ports. Those to the Mediterranean begin at London, take in Barcelona, Tarragona and Valencia, and terminate at Liverpool or London. Voyages starting in London, Liverpool and Hull take her to the Baltic, where she typically calls at several ports, including Gothenburg and Pillau. The voyage pattern strongly suggests that, despite ownership since new by the General Iron Screw Collier Company Limited, she was in the liner trade, probably chartered by the voyage, and possibly bringing fruit home from the Mediterranean.

Thus, with the *John Bowes* Palmers had built a very versatile type of steamer which was by no means confined to the east coast coal trade. In the decades which followed, iron shipbuilding grew enormously on the Tyne, Wear, and Tees and to an even greater extent on the Clyde. The products of these rivers were frequently cargo ships up to about 250 feet in length, the pioneer tramp steamers and cargo liners. Were the former, with their single decks, relatively large hatches, and water ballast arrangements, any

In 1906, when owned in Sweden as *Transit*, the 54-year-old collier was photographed passing Palmers' yard. Her rig had been further reduced. Note the letter T on the funnel for owners Red. Aktieb. Transport. *[Author's collection]*

Photographed at Santander in October 1930, the 78-year old hull, now named *Valentin Fierro*, has what was probably its last drydocking. Her rig has been reduced further, and she now has an enclosed bridge. *[National Maritime Museum P49624-5]*

more than enlargements and developments of the *John Bowes?* Engines were usually placed amidships to lessen stresses on their larger iron hulls, and the number of holds increased with length. These differences tended to mask the parallels between collier and tramp, but the similarities are much more marked between *John Bowes* and the present-day successor of the steam tramp, the bulk carrier. The steam collier built for the east coast trade grew larger and larger. The last of these were substantial ships, almost 340 feet in overall length, for example the series built for the Central Electricity Authority which finished with the *Sir Johnstone Wright* (3,382/1955) and those for North Thames Gas Board, ending with the *Thomas Goulden* (3,332/1955). Their features were those of the present-day bulk carrier: large hatches, cargo space divided into a number of holds, lack of cargo gear, water ballast arrangements, and engines moved aft once again to minimise the length (and vulnerability of) the propellor shaft and to provide clear holds. As a photographic survey of steam colliers will seek to illustrate in *Record* 21, this type of ship, and by extension the much larger bulk carrier of today, is simply an application of the principles embodied in the *John Bowes* 150 years ago.

No other author has been bold enough to describe the *John Bowes* as the progenitor of the ocean-going tramp, but equally none gives the honour to any other vessel. Robin Craig treats the technical developments which the screw collier pioneered as being applicable to vessels large and small in other bulk trades, and undoubtedly the practical shipbuilder and naval architect of the mid-nineteenth century would not see water ballast, unobstructed holds and more efficient engines as applicable only to the east coast coal trade. A paper on the steam collier by Allen, delivered to the Institution of Civil Engineers in February 1855, less than three years after the launch of *John Bowes,* has a lengthy discussion on the use of steam colliers to supply distant coaling stations, and this may well be the first time serious consideration had been given to the use of an ocean-going steam bulk carrier. John Scott Russell's notebooks, preserved in the library of the Science Museum in London, also contain notes and calculations on the building and running of a line of screw steamers to run between Liverpool and Trieste. If the steam tramp and the bulk carrier did indeed evolve directly from the screw collier of the 1850s, the *John Bowes* may well be one of the most important vessels ever built.

What if?

If *Record* may be allowed to flirt with contrafactualism, it may be asked would shipping history have been much different if Palmers had not built the *John Bowes?* The five prior experiments described above confirm that the principles of combining an iron hull with a steam engine were appreciated by other collier builders and owners. The north east coal owner Lord Londonderry - who later built up a considerable fleet of steamers and his own harbour at Seaham - is said to have been contemplating ordering a screw collier in 1852. The ballast problem was also being imaginatively and energetically tackled. John Scott Russell, for instance, pointed out that ballast tanks represented a loss of valuable cargo space. The holds of the colliers *Eagle* 480/1853), *Falcon* (354/1853) and *Hawk* (487/1854) built at Russell's Poplar yard were fitted with collapsible canvas 'ballast bags', but these were easily damaged when loading the coal cargo resulting in leaks, even when timbers were laid over the bags. In another solution, Scott Russell's *Imperial* (482/1857) had a complete hold amidships which could be filled with water ballast, but apparently it was not sufficiently leak-proof and placed an undue strain on the hull when filled. Double-bottom ballast tanks remained supreme, but it was such an obvious development that, if

McIntyre had not devised it, some other designer would sooner or later have hit upon the idea. Thus, even without the Palmers, another yard, possibly on the Thames, would almost certainly have developed an efficient steam collier during the 1850s, pioneering developments that rescued the north east coal trade and may well have anticipated the modern bulk carrier.

Although the steam collier would probably have still been born, shipbuilding on the Tyne may not have developed to the extent it did without the *John Bowes.* Palmer's success in immediately attracting orders for further colliers allowed the family to construct an enterprise that, in its scope, for many years dwarfed all other iron shipbuilders, including Scott Russell who was soon to be embroiled in the awesome difficulties attending the construction of Brunel's *Great Eastern* (18,915/1858). Palmers quickly moved on to bigger and much more complex vessels than the humble collier; pioneering ironclad warships such as HMS *Terror* of 1856, completed in just three months; and building ocean-going cargo and passenger ships such as Royal Mail's *Connaught* of 1860, and being instrumental in developing the oil tanker, with the *Vaderland* of 1872, the first steamer built as a tanker. The Jarrow yard became a remarkable industrial complex, taking in annually around 18,000 tons of iron ore delivered by Palmers' own coasters from the deposits they exploited in north Yorkshire, and turning out some of the world's most sophisticated steam ships. Other Tyneside builders - notably Swan, Hunter - may have eventually passed them in prestige, but Palmers showed Tyneside, and probably the world, what iron shipbuilding could achieve. By the time their yards at Jarrow and Hebburn closed or were sold in the 1930s, they had delivered over one thousand ships, ranging in size and complexity from tugs to battleships. This owed everything to the success of the *John Bowes.*

JOHN BOWES 1852-1898 Iron
O.N. 26276 *1852:* 485g 375n 148.9 x 25.7 x 15.6 feet
1871: 437g 270n 150.0 x 25.7 x 15.6 feet
2-cyl. by R. Stephenson and Co., Newcastle-upon-Tyne; 9 knots, 70 NHP.
1862: I. 2-cyl. by Thompson, Boyd and Co., Newcastle-upon-Tyne; 70 NHP.
1883: C. 2-cyl. by M. Paul and Co., Dumbarton; 60 HP.
30.6.1852: Launched by Palmers Brothers and Co., Jarrow (Yard No. 2).
19.7.1852: Completed.
24.7.1852: Registered in the ownership of James J. Allport, Manchester (21/64); James E. MacConnell, Wolverton (21/64); Charles M. Palmer, Newcastle-upon-Tyne (11/64); George Palmer junior, Jarrow (11/64) as JOHN BOWES.
20.11.1860: Owners became James E. MacConnell, Wolverton; Charles M. Palmer, Newcastle-on-Tyne; and George Palmer junior, Jarrow.
28.3.1868: Owner became Charles M. Palmer, Newcastle-on-Tyne.
23.4.1873: Registered in the ownership of Benjamin G. Barnett, trading as Barnett Brothers, London.
3.6.1896: Sold to the John Bowes Steamship Co. Ltd. (John Mackenzie, manager), Dublin.
19.4.1898: Sold by order of the Admiralty Marshall to Charles H. Pile, London.
18.5.1898: Register closed when sold to Frithjof Ohlsen, Fredriksvaern, Norway and renamed SPEC.
1900: Sold to Red. Aktieb. Transport (J.E. Olsen, manager), Gothenburg, Sweden and renamed TRANSIT.
12.1908: Sold to T. de Ybargary, Bilbao, Spain for £2,000 and renamed CAROLINA.
1919: Sold to Compañia Naviera Fierros, Oviedo, Spain and renamed VALENTIN FIERRO.
1931: Sold to Federico G. Fierro, San Esteban de Pravia, Spain.
1932: Renamed VILLA SELGAS.
13.10.1933: Sprang a leak and foundered during a gale off San Antolin, Rivadesella whilst on a voyage from Bilbao to San Esteban Pravia with a cargo of iron ore. Her crew was saved.

INDEX TO RECORD 17 TO 20

Record 17: pp.1-64; *Record 18*: 65-128; *Record 19*: pp. 129-192; *Record 20*: 193-264.

Index of articles

Index of ships

Elstree Grange at Swansea - see page 198. *[World Ship Society]*